fresh Flower arranging

fresh
Flower
arranging

Mark Welford and Stephen Wicks

DK

LONDON, NEW YORK, MUNICH,
MELBOURNE, DELHI

Editor Susannah Steel
Photography Carolyn Barber

Project Editor Andrew Roff
Project Art Editor William Hicks
US Editor Rebecca Warren
Designers Miranda Harvey, Simon Murrell
Managing Editor Dawn Henderson
Managing Art Editors Christine Keilty,
Marianne Markham
Senior Jackets Creative Nicola Powling
Senior Presentations Creative
Caroline de Souza
Senior Production Editor Jennifer Murray
Senior Production Controller Alice Sykes
Creative Technical Support
Sonia Charbonnier

First American edition, 2011

Published in the United States by
DK Publishing
375 Hudson Street
New York, New York 10014

11 12 13 14 15 10 9 8 7 6 5 4 3 2 1

176539—February 2011

Copyright © 2011
Dorling Kindersley Limited

Published in Great Britain by Dorling Kindersley Limited.

A catalog record for this book
is available from the Library of Congress.

ISBN 978-0-7566-5859-5

Printed and bound in China by Toppan

Discover more at **www.dk.com**

CONTENTS

INTRODUCTION

Stephen (right) and I opened our shop, Bloomsbury Flowers, in London's Covent Garden, which is close to the Royal Opera House where we both danced many times.

As with ballet, technique is all-important in floristry. Learning how to arrange flowers in a hand-tied bouquet was one of the first skills we had to master.

We met in 1970 in London, England at White Lodge, the Royal Ballet Lower School, and although we were a school year apart we became friends. In the late 1970s we joined the Sadler's Wells Royal Ballet, which was later to become known as the Birmingham Royal Ballet.

As we neared our "sell-by date" as dancers in the 1990s, we discussed what we would do when we retired. Stephen has always loved flowers and had already arranged the flowers for a friend's wedding. Although I was a keen gardener, I knew little about the world of cut flowers, so it was somewhat of a surprise when Stephen suggested the idea of opening a flower shop together: "All we need are some buckets, a cold tap, and a pair of scissors!"

We applied for support from the Dancers' Career Development (DCD), a charity that helps ex-dancers make the transition into a new career. With the DCD's generous support, we were able to open the doors of Bloomsbury Flowers in Covent Garden in December 1994. We made a promise to ourselves that we would not compromise on the quality of our flowers, but also ensure that they always provide the best value.

Our mission is to make our flowers as theatrical as possible while following our motto of "less is more" by ensuring that even the simplest bunch of tulips leaves the shop looking exquisite, unpretentious, and beautifully wrapped. We are always confident that once a customer removes the wrapping, the flowers will still look fantastic. We have even managed to change the style of the presentation bouquets handed to ballerinas at the end of a performance at the Royal Opera House, London: we have created a unique way of wrapping the flowers so they are not encased in cellophane (which reflects the stage lights so the flowers can't be seen) and can be enjoyed by the audiences, too.

Our ballet background has provided us with some invaluable experience when it comes to floristry. Timing was a fundamental part of our preparation and performance on stage every night, and we have since found that timing is an important aspect of being a successful florist. For example, we are always aware of how long it takes to make up a hand-tied bouquet, install arrangements throughout a hotel, and prepare flowers for an event so they will look their best. We also know that good technique is fundamental to being a confident ballet dancer—and the same is true for floristry. In this book you will learn valuable basic techniques that will enable you to make all the arrangements featured, and inspire you to try creative designs of your own.

We have taken time to decide which designs we should include in this book; they're inspired not only by life, but by things that you may find in your own home. We have also focused on surroundings, color, and containers, as these are all essential elements to consider when putting together an arrangement. Being aware of the environment in which the flowers will be positioned is important: what works well in opulent surroundings will not necessarily look as good in a venue with a minimalist look. Color is of paramount importance, and one aspect of floristry that can be a little overwhelming; it's important to know how to work with color in your designs. We have learnt from each other over the years, as Stephen, if left to his own devices, prefers to work in tonal colors, whereas I always lean toward mixed colors. Containers, too, play a vital part in floral design, and over the years we have built up a large collection. They range from clear vases and galvanized buckets to wooden boxes tied with seagrass, antique wine crates, jewelry boxes, colored glass containers, and stoneware containers, many of which you will see through the book.

The aim of this book is to inspire, not intimidate, and we hope that our style will become your style, too. Whether it involves learning a simple technique to arrange single blooms in a container or using insider tips to create a large-scale display, this book is about making what is already beautiful even more so.

The shop interior is our stage, and the set changes almost daily with deliveries of fresh flowers and foliage. We love the way flowers can instantly transform an environment.

We believe that attention to detail and presentation is everything; our simple but stylish packaging for our flowers allows them to speak for themselves.

SECTION ONE
PRINCIPLES

This section explains everything you need to know to pick the right flowers in the most suitable colors, prepare and arrange them skilfully, and position them for the best effect.

LESS IS MORE

Our philosophy is all about "less is more." There is no need for complicated tricks and overpowering displays to make your flowers look good; often, the simplest of arrangements can have the most wonderful impact. To make fantastic flower arrangements, you just need to follow some simple rules and think about how to be more creative with, for example, the mixed bunch of flowers that you have bought from a limited selection on sale, or gathered from your garden. Rather than following the standard approach of putting the flowers straight into a vase together, the different elements can be separated into individual containers so that each becomes a beautiful statement in itself.

MIXED FLOWERS
Roses and gypsophila are typically sold and arranged together. It's not wrong to do this, but it doesn't show either variety of flower at its best. The fluffy gypsophila doesn't enhance the dense, compact rose petals in the right way, and together they look unexciting and dreary.

CREATIVE SOLUTION
By separating the two varieties of flower and placing them in different containers, the gypsophila becomes a delicate cloud of tiny flowers that has an airy, dreamy quality while the deep, rich tones of the red roses resonate together to look exquisite—our "less is more" theory.

SPACE

Before you even think about choosing a container, a color scheme, and flowers and foliage, consider the space in which you will position your arrangement. When we are asked to design flowers for an occasion—be it for an office or entrance hall, a formal dinner, an intimate hotel room, or a wedding party—we always visit the venue first if we are unfamiliar with the surroundings. We need to make sure that we understand the proportions of the room, and exactly where the flowers will be placed.

WIDE

If you have a large, spacious room to work with—perhaps a grand entrance area, or a large reception room, where the flowers may be seen from several sides—one big, all-round statement piece will work much better than a few small, insignificant displays. Choose a substantial vase or container and fill it with an abundance of lush, opulent, seasonal flowers. It's also worth thinking about what the arrangement will stand on: a plinth or side table will influence how tall the flowers and foliage should be.

NARROW

A windowsill, mantelpiece, desk, or shelf may seem a difficult spot to fill with flowers, but a long, slim container filled with bulbs or potted herbs will suit the space perfectly. This type of design will also be long-lasting, because bulbs and herbs with roots will grow well if there is enough natural light in the room.

LOW

It is important to remember that people need to see each other above the flowers if you are designing an arrangement for a coffee table or as a table centerpiece for an office meeting room or a dinner table. Choose low arrangements—simple designs often work best—and make sure the flowers complement the container. The flowers will also last longer, as their stems will be short.

TALL

A tall arrangement will create the right impact if you are working in a high-ceilinged room, an entrance hall, or need to draw the eye upward. Displays for this space work best if they are not overly fussy, so keep them quite minimal, striking, or architectural in design—perhaps with just a few carefully chosen flowers. A tall vase is a must.

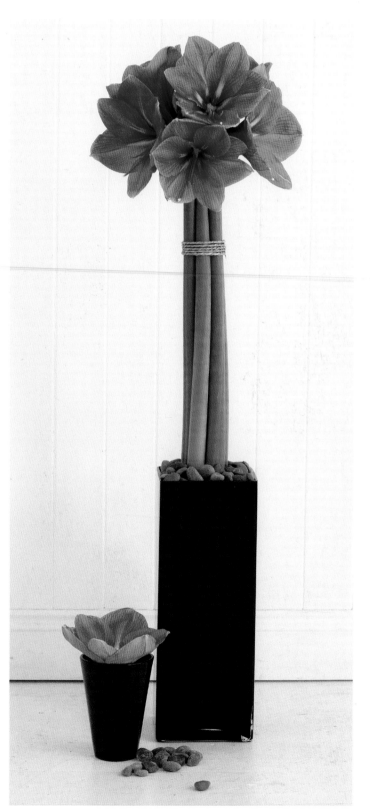

COLOR

Perhaps the most powerful component of any flower arrangement is its color scheme. Color is emotive because it has an immediate impact on our senses, and it can communicate a mood or a message almost instantly. There is a spectacular array of colors in nature—from subtle, harmonious tones to striking, intense, iridescent hues—and flowers encapsulate much of that dynamic range and diversity. Some basic principles about color theory can be applied to flower arranging to help you choose the right flowers and foliage to make designs that create an inviting atmosphere and are stylish to look at.

COLOR THEORY

In color theory, the three primary colors—red, blue, and yellow—can be mixed in different combinations to create a spectrum of other colors. These combinations are arranged in a simple circle, or color wheel, to show their relationship to each other. This color wheel (right), composed of flowers and foliage, shows how these relationships work in practice.

WHAT WORKS

Colors that lie near or next to each other on the color wheel contain elements of the primary colors they sit between, so they go well together. For example, purple harmonizes well with blue and red because it sits in between them on the color wheel. Each color also has a tonal value—a light and dark version of that color—that also creates harmony, but can influence the mood of an arrangement to make it warm or cool, or gentle or intense. So pale purple, blue, and pink blooms convey a light, gentle mood, while strong, darker tones of these colors are more intense and dramatic. Foliage, with its different textures and subtle variations of green, also helps different colors to blend well. Colors that sit opposite each other

FLOWER COLOR WHEEL
This color wheel reveals how colors influence each other when they are placed near, next to, or opposite each other.

Primary colors
Red, one of the three primary colors, sits equidistant from the other two primary colors, blue and yellow, on the color wheel. They are the key anchors of the color wheel and, mixed together in different proportions, they create all other colors.

Harmonious colors
Colors that sit next to or near each other on the color wheel, such as pinks and purples, make a visually pleasing combination when arranged in a mixed display.

Contrasting colors
Colors that sit directly opposite each other on the color wheel are known as complementary, or contrasting, colors, as they appear more powerful together than they do apart. For example, blue and orange flowers enhance one another when mixed together in a design.

on the color wheel have a powerful effect on one another. In nature, some complementary colors enhance each other, and can look better together than apart. For instance, the flowers in a red and green design, or a pink and lime-green bouquet, look more vibrant, saturated, and pure when placed together than if arranged separately.

THE RULES IN PRACTICE
Although there are not necessarily any colors that shouldn't go together, some combinations work better than others. For example, yellow and orange are a good combination, as are purple, red, and pink. A good guideline is to limit yourself to three or four harmonious colors or two complementary colors; a multi-colored arrangement can impair your visual pleasure, as it is too confusing on the eye. It's also worth bearing in mind that a mass of one variety of flower in just one color can create more impact if it is arranged well. Before you buy any flowers, look at the space in which you will position your arrangement and think about which flower colors go best with the color scheme of your surroundings so you can create the most pleasing impact.

USING WHITE IN ARRANGEMENTS
White flowers should be used carefully in arrangements because white can dominate some colors and dull others. White and red, for example, are both hard colors that can jar together; we prefer to use cream and maroon flowers that, when teamed with foliage, make a softer, more luxurious mix. However, we often use white flowers on their own or with green foliage, or we combine them with cream blooms, which soften and enhance them. And when teamed with a limited palette of harmonious colors, such as blue, purple, and green, white flowers can take on an almost iridescent, shimmering quality amid the other blooms.

ESSENTIAL CONTAINERS

Every flower design must suit the occasion and the surroundings it is intended for, so decide on your container first before you select the flowers: think about the impression you want to create and consider the size, shape, and color of the container in order to get the right look. This selection of vases represents the four essential shapes you need in your collection; with this limited choice you can create a wonderful variety of arrangements and show off the flowers to their best effect.

FISHBOWL

This globe shape is good for highlighting the beauty of just a few blooms by curling and swirling them within the curved contours of the bowl. It is also ideal for displaying tall-stemmed hand-tied bouquets that require a dramatic edge.

CUBE VASE

A square-shaped vase is perfect for displaying a mass of one type of flower, and ideal for smaller, compact arrangements with short-stemmed flowers. The straight sides of this vase enforce a geometric framework onto the blooms, giving them a modern look.

COLUMN VASE

A straight-sided vase such as this can "contain" the flowers within it, so you can use it to create sculptural or uniform arrangements. Its extended height allows displays of tall-stemmed flowers to be well supported so they don't droop, but you can also use it for contemporary designs, such as a compact ball or "bomb" of large, domed flowers that sits on the rim of the vase.

FLARED VASE

This vase allows flowers and foliage to fall naturally at pleasing angles to create a fan shape, and it can display a wide variety of flowers clearly in a large arrangement. Its tapered base also limits the spread of their stems, ensuring that any displays requiring an extravagant flourish or an element of drama or impact have added height.

CONTAINERS FOR EVERY OCCASION

This selection shows something of the variety of colors, textures, shapes, and sizes of vases and containers that can inspire your flower design. Choose a container that lends itself to the flowers, and vice versa. Any non-watertight containers can be adapted using cellophane or cut-down plastic water bottles. If you can't find the right container, you always have the option of using floral foam (pp44–47) or arranging the flowers as a hand-tied bouquet (pp40–43).

ORANGE FISHBOWL ↓
Neon-colored globe-shaped glass vase, best used for modern domed flower designs.

EPHEMERA VASE →
Column vase covered in old, torn papers to create texture and interest with a mixed selection of flowers.

↓ PINK FLOWERPOT
Flared glass vase that lends a modern air to a simple small vase arrangement.

↓ METAL VASE
Classic version of a flared vase that suits traditional displays.

↑ SMALL BUCKET
Modern galvanized bucket that looks great with a mass of one variety of short-stemmed blooms.

MINI CUBE ↑
Tiny version of a cube vase for individual blooms.

↑ TARTLET PANS ↑
Use as place settings with short-stemmed single flower heads.

FOOD CAN ↑
Empty can makes an attractive flared vase for a potted bulb.

↑ COCONUT SHELL
Treat like an opaque fishbowl for minimal, modern displays of exotic blooms.

↑ METAL URN
Use for miniature versions of flared vase displays with classic selection of mixed flowers.

OPAQUE COLUMN VASE ↓
Patterned column glass vases in neutral colors look good with just a few long-stemmed statement flowers.

POTTERY VASE ↓
A patterned, flared vase shows off most flower arrangements well.

TERRA-COTTA CUBE ↓
Non-porous container has a cut-down water bottle placed inside to make it watertight.

↑ **ANTIQUE VASE**
Glass vase with a small neck to display just a few short-stemmed blooms.

POTTERY PITCHER ↑
Ideal for a few flowers with their stems cut short.

TEA LIGHT HOLDER →
Useful for multiple small, informal displays.

CUP AND SAUCER →
Porcelain teacups can hold single flowers.

↑ **OVAL TROUGH**
Painted terra-cotta pot for low floral foam displays.

FLOWER SHAPES

The enormously diverse varieties of flower we see around us can be classified into a limited range of flower shapes. Recognizing the most basic of these shapes is extremely helpful in understanding which types of flowers you should select and how they work best in particular arrangements. Another way to understand this is that there are no "wrong" flowers, but there is a wrong and a right way to use them. The eight flower shapes we have selected here are those that we think are among the most attractive and useful for flower arranging.

FLAT-TOPPED (trachelium) →
Most flat-topped flowers are quite large, but the many tiny flowers arranged in clusters on short stalks that form these flower heads make them look airy and delicate in appearance.
Good for This flower shape is useful for hand-tied bouquets, because it helps to form the required dome shape. It also provides textural interest and detail in both large and small designs.
Flowers Trachelium, Queen Anne's lace, dill

SPEAR →
(delphinium)
Clusters of small flowers on short stalks growing at the top of a stem form a typical spear flower shape. With so many individual flowers on one stem, these flowers are full of color and interest.
Good for Flowers with elongated stems, such as molucella and delphiniums, provide structure, form, and necessary height in large vases or structural designs.
Flowers Delphiniums, molucella, orchids, gentiana, liatris, lupins, foxgloves, lilacs, Solomon's seal

DOME (hydrangea) →
Large and small domed flowers are real "feature" flowers that provide substance and focus in an arrangement. The flower heads are usually quite dense and provide a strong injection of color in a design.
Good for This flower shape is suitable for large displays and minimalist designs.
Flowers Hydrangeas, most celosias, chrysanthemums

← REGULAR
(gerbera)
Flowers with the same-shaped petals in a simple circular shape around its center have what is called radial symmetry: whichever way you divide a regular flower, it has two or three similar parts.
Good for These flowers are adaptable: they can be used on their own in striking designs or as a repeat pattern in a larger arrangement.
Flowers Gerberas, sunflowers, marguerites, daffodils, narcissi, anemones

← GLOBE (allium)

The perfectly round shape of globe flowers means they look most impressive *en masse*, and usually work best in a minimalist design of just one or two types of flower.

Good for These flowers work well in modern and sculptural designs, especially if the strong, straight stems of flowers such as alliums are left as long as possible.

Flowers Alliums, tulips, protea

ROSETTE (rose) ↓

The geometric rosette shape of some flowers makes them ideal for large and small arrangements alike.

Good for These flowers attract the eye easily and so can be used as feature flowers in a mixed display or on their own in a minimalist design.

Flowers Single roses, globe artichokes, ranunculas, peonies, dahlias, carnations

SPRAY (eryngium) →

With their branching stems and large quantity of flower heads, spray flowers are adaptable, and are ideal for mixed arrangements.

Good for If the flower heads are left on their single main stem, they can be used to reinforce the fan shape of a vase display, or provide a mass of color and interest in hand-tied bouquets. They can also be cut down to provide numerous shorter-stemmed flowers in floral foam designs.

Flowers Eryngium, lilies, spray roses, lisianthus, astrantia

← SPIRE (veronica)

A spire shape has small, stalkless flowers at the tip of a long stem. The flowers open in sequence, usually from the bottom, which helps to create its tapering shape.

Good for These shapes contrast well with softer-petaled flowers, and are useful for breaking the smooth outlines of a domed bouquet or floral foam design.

Flowers Veronica, stocks, antirrhinums, grape hyacinths, hyacinths, lily of the valley, lavender

FOLIAGE TYPES

The aim of using foliage in an arrangement is to provide texture, extra color, shape, and proportion: whether you design a front-facing arrangement or a three-dimensional display, foliage will help to give it the necessary height, width, depth, and interest that it needs in order to look balanced and substantial. Some foliage works better in large arrangements to fill out and shape the design, while sculptural grasses create interest and height. Other—usually year-round—foliage works better in small designs to give added detail and color. Ultimately, however, the foliage that you choose for an arrangement will always depend on its seasonal or year-round availability.

YEAR-ROUND FOLIAGE

With the exception of ruscus, year-round foliage tends to be short and so is best used for medium-sized and compact arrangements. Choose foliage such as pittosporum, salal, eucalyptus, bear grass, snake grass, leather leaf, and black tie and green tie leaves.

← RUSCUS
These attractive feathery leaves on long curved stems add a delicate texture to a design.

← SALAL
This foliage is a dense filler best used for small designs and bouquets.

EUCALYPTUS →
The unusual silver-green leaves, pleasant scent, and handsome arching stems of eucalyptus enhance the shape of a design and add an extra flourish.

SEASONAL FOLIAGE
The tall, straight stems of cotinus, forsythia, privet, red robin, white leaf, and rhododendron are ideal for large displays, and any side shoots can be used at the edges of a design, or in a compact arrangement. Hebe, berried ivy, senecio, hypericum, and alchemilla are best-suited for compact arrangements. Condition seasonal foliage well, or it will quickly droop.

← PRIVET
Tall and dramatic, privet provides an effective backdrop for long-stemmed flowers.

← ALCHEMILLA
With its unusual lime-green color and lacy appearance, alchemilla is ideal for breaking up a dense mass of flowers. It is pretty enough to be used like a flower in some designs.

RED ROBIN →
This red-stemmed foliage adds a rich color accent to a fall display.

SHAPES AT WORK

These pages illustrate the different ways in which you can put the eight basic flower shapes into practice. Some displays use just one shape *en masse* to give a simple or dramatic result, while others are used to create a particular effect in mixed arrangements with seasonal or all-year foliage.

DOME

Hydrangea and celosia flowers are dominant blooms in these designs, and as a result their strong domed shape dictates the shape of the display.

FLORAL CUPCAKES pp122–23
Including hydrangea with roses and peonies adds weight and drama to this design, and echoes the shapes of the full-blown peonies.

FRUIT CUBE pp164–65
Dense-headed, textural red and green celosias create interest and impact when arranged as a seasonal hand-tied bouquet and placed in a vase.

HYDRANGEA BALL pp140–41
Dome-shaped flowers often work well on their own in a display, as this curved fishbowl of domed hydrangea flower heads with short stems shows.

FLAT-TOPPED

Flowers such as trachelium and dill can be used in both tall displays and in low floral foam arrangements to define shape and add texture.

WINTER WEDDING TABLE CENTERPIECE p202
These frosty trachelium are a perfect foil for the other flowers: their abundance of small, dainty flower heads break up the intense clusters of freesia and rose petals.

SUMMER LONG AND LOW pp114–17
The dark dill flowers in this design create a smooth contour and help to define its shape. They also add depth of color to what could be an all-too-pink display.

VEGETABLE AND FRUIT BOUQUET pp174–75
Using purple trachelium in this quirky, hand-tied bouquet helps to inject color and texture in what is otherwise a mainly green and quite dense design.

REGULAR
Flowers that have a regular shape work well in many designs, and add symmetry to minimalist arrangements.

GERBERA IN LINES pp248–49
This display is a perfect example of how to use regular flowers in a modern, architectural design to create uniformity and order.

NARCISSI TREE pp80–81
Using these narcissi to create a topiary tree in effect creates another regular shape: the gathered blooms look like one large flower.

SUNFLOWER VASE pp156–57
Although this arrangement uses different varieties of sunflowers—all of which are a regular shape—it still has impact because of the contrasting colors.

SPEAR
These tall, spear-shaped flowers add drama and often height to traditional and contemporary designs alike.

DELPHINIUMS AND HYDRANGEAS IN BLUE pp144–45
The tall delphiniums in this modern vase display add height and drama to the short-stemmed hydrangeas.

LILAC GARDEN PITCHER pp102–103
This is an example of how to use a shorter spear flower, such as garden lilac, to add texture and interest to this simple vase design.

TOWERING LIATRIS pp228–29
An arrangement such as this uses just one variety of spear-shaped flower to make a strong statement in a tall column vase.

GLOBE

Proteas, alliums, and tulips are all flowers that retain their inherent round shape well in an arrangement once their petals have opened.

GELATIN MOLD MIX pp70–71
The tulips in this mixed arrangement show off their globe shape beautifully against the other small, spire-shaped flowers.

TULIPS IN A BOWL pp66–67
A fishbowl display is a lovely way to enjoy these glamorous French parrot tulips. Their round heads contrast well with the long, razor-sharp grasses.

AUTUMN BOUQUET pp160–61
Globe-shaped varieties of the exotic protea flower look spectacular in a compact hand-tied bouquet, as they echo the rounded shape of the arrangement.

SPRAY

The great thing about spray flowers is that they are versatile; they work well in many designs, including hand-tied bouquets and floral foam.

COUNTRY SUMMER WEDDING TABLE CENTERPIECE pp134–35
In this floral foam design the spray roses are ideal as a filler, and add interest to the arrangement.

WINTER BRIDAL BOUQUET p201
The white spray roses in this bouquet blend well with a mass of white freesias to provide a backdrop for the large single roses that are the main feature.

ASIAN FAN pp234–35
In this modern design, spray rose stems are cut short to echo the shape created by tall calla lilies, and provide an intense burst of color at the heart of the design.

SPIRE

Spire flowers are often quite delicate, but their pointed flower heads add height and interest to mixed flower arrangements.

SUMMER HARMONY pp112–13
The small purple spires of veronica in this front-facing display soften its edges and balance out the large, round, eye-catching hydrangeas and roses.

CREAM BASKET pp120–21
Stocks are used here for their scent and shape, which breaks up and adds height to a long and low design. This helps to give it a more relaxed, informal look.

SUMMER BOUQUET pp124–25
This hand-tied bunch includes deep pink lysimachia, which have been deliberately left long to make the bunch more informal and less rounded.

ROSETTE

These flowers, with petals that open in a rosette, circular shape, make great feature blooms. Some varieties, such as carnations, work well *en masse*.

SPRING BOUQUET pp82–83
These orange ranunculas, set among other spring flowers, contrast beautifully with the grape hyacinths. They are grouped in threes for a stronger look.

GREEN BOUQUET pp236–37
Roses are a typical rosette flower, and here they hold their own—even when mixed with large, brightly colored flowers such as these anthuriums.

CARNATION SCULPTURE pp246–47
A large quantity of carnation flower heads pressed into a floral foam ball together create a dense geometric shape that echoes the shape of a single carnation.

EQUIPMENT

There are certain tools and a limited amount of equipment that you need to condition flowers, arrange them properly, and maintain them. These are the essential supplies you need to make all the arrangements in this book. Work in a cool room, sweep up leaves and stems from the floor as you work so you don't slip on them, and use a large bucket to condition the flowers and foliage.

CLEAR TAPE ↓
Use to bind split stems, make grids across vase tops, and wrap bouquets.

HAND MISTER ↓
Use to refresh or revive blooms with a fine mist of water.

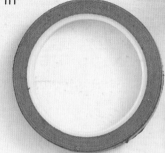

FLORIST'S TAPE ↑
Use to bind floral foam to a plastic tray or bowl.

STEM TAPE ↑
Use to cover and seal individually wired flower and foliage stems.

STERILIZING TABLETS →
Add to a vase or container of water to kill bacteria and help to keep the water clear.

PEARL PINS ↓
For boutonnieres and pinning ribbons in place.

PIN CUSHION ↑
Necessary for arranging stems at precise angles (pp234–35).

← SHALLOW BOWL
Shallow plastic bowl designed to hold enough floral foam for a small arrangement.

PAINTBRUSH ↓
For dusting any pollen off flower petals.

MOUNTING PUTTY →
Useful for attaching fabric and coverings to containers.

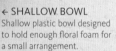

VIAL ↑
For keeping single-stemmed flowers fresh before being presented.

BOTTLE BRUSH ↘
For cleaning vases and containers.

← DEEP BOWL
Plastic bowl that holds enough floral foam for a large front-facing display.

22 GAUGE WIRE ↑
Suitable for wiring larger flower stems, ribbons, and other equipment.

ROSE WIRES ↑
Use for wiring smaller-stemmed flowers and boutonnieres.

LONG-STEMMED VIAL ↑
Attach to short-stemmed flowers in mixed designs.

GARDEN STAKES IN VARIOUS SIZES ↓
Useful for providing support and placing ingredients in position.

RUBBER BANDS ↓
Useful for making up bunches of finer foliage such as bear grass.

RAFFIA ↑
Ideal for binding hand-tied bouquets and arranged stems.

GARDEN STRING ↑
A suitable alternative to raffia.

PLASTIC BOTTLE ↓
Cut-down plastic bottle to hold flowers in water in non-watertight containers.

↑ DECORATIVE COLORED REEL WIRES
Wires in various colors and thicknesses to bind the stems of flowers or add decorative details.

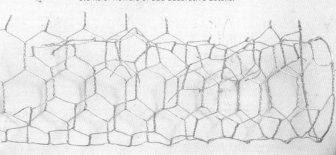

CHICKEN WIRE ↑
Mold to fit and place in an opaque vase or container to hold the stems of an arrangement in place.

FLORAL FOAM BLOCK AND TRAY →
Use for medium-sized floral foam arrangements.

FLORIST'S SCISSORS ↓
Ideal for conditioning and trimming flowers and thin-stemmed foliage.

CRAFT KNIFE →
Use to condition flowers and cut and trim soaked blocks of floral foam.

SHEARS →
Use to trim and split woody-stemmed foliage and thick-stemmed flowers.

CHOOSING AND PREPARING

Select the best-quality flowers available from your local florist or grower, and stay as seasonal as possible with your choices. Depending on the occasion, choose blooms that are still in bud or already beginning to open, and as a general rule, buy a maximum of four to five types of flower in three or four harmonious, or two complementary, colors. If scent is important, ask your florist for advice before you buy and check if the flowers have a light or a stronger, heady scent—it may have an impact on where you intend to place the flowers, as some scents can be overpowering in small rooms.

WHEN TO BUY FLOWERS

For arrangements that will last longer at home, buy flowers such as lilies, amaryllis, roses, ranunculas, and tulips while they are still in bud. However, if you need flowers as a short-term effect for a special occasion such as a wedding, buy flowers that are already beginning to open up so they will look their best on the day.

HEALTHY ROSES

To check whether the roses you want to buy are really fresh and will last well in an arrangement, gently squeeze a few of the flower heads near the base where the petals meet the sepals. If the roses are firm, rather than spongy and soft, they are a better choice and will have a longer life span.

Choose flowers such as lilies with their buds in various stages of opening; they shouldn't all be completely closed and neither should they all be almost open.

An older rose has a soft base and tired-looking petals.

A fresh rose has a firm base and tighter, crisp-looking petals.

INSIDER TIPS

• Remove pollen from flowers such as lilies (see right) to prevent stains on petals or clothing, and prevent allergy sufferers from experiencing any symptoms. Lily pollen is poisonous to cats and dogs so remove it if you own one.

• If you use a clear vase, add a sterilizing tablet or stir flower food into the water and dissolve before adding flowers. This will keep the water clear and kill any bacteria.

• To encourage buds to open, take off more leaves. With fewer leaves on the stems, more water and nutrients pass to the flower head. To encourage lilies to open, put the stems in warm water, let the water cool, and repeat.

REMOVING POLLEN
Gently pull the pollen-laden stamens from the center of the flower with your thumb and forefinger. If you miss a flower and the stamens become powdery, pinch the stamens out in the same way and dust off any stray pollen with a paintbrush.

CONDITIONING

It's important to condition your flowers and foliage as soon as you have bought them so that they remain in peak condition for as long as possible. Strip the excess leaves from the stems (below left) and split the ends of any woody stems (below right). Place all the flower and foliage stems in a bucket of deep cold water for a long drink for about an hour before you start to trim the stems and arrange the flowers—this will help to hydrate the flowers and ensure that they will bloom while they are still fresh. If the flowers have enough to drink at this stage, they shouldn't need quite so much water once they have been arranged in a display.

STRIPPING STEMS

2 Leave a few leaves near the top of each stem, but remove any leaves that might stand in water. Foliage often has shorter stems than flowers, so cut off lower side shoots to create longer stems.

1 Lay the flowers and foliage out on a table. Take one stem, stand it upright on a table, and run a craft knife down the sides of the stem to remove any thorns and unwanted leaves.

SPLITTING STEMS

2 Split the ends of woody stems such as roses, lilac, and cultivated guelder with florist's scissors. This increases the surface area of the plant cells in these thicker foliage and flower stems so they take in more water.

1 Make a diagonal cut about 1in (2.5cm) from the base of each stem to encourage the stems to take up more water and hydrate the flower heads.

MAINTENANCE

To prolong the life and look of your flowers, change the water—or mist floral foam displays and moisten the foam—every other day. If you use flower food, change the water every four or five days. Stems in vase arrangements also need to be recut every few days, as their ends soon become waterlogged and mushy, restricting the flow of water up to the flower and causing the flowers to droop and lose their petals more quickly. Recutting each stem rehydrates the flower heads and keeps them looking fresh. There are also other ways to revive particular flowers and neaten split stems if your display begins to look a little tired.

MISTING

If it is a hot day when you prepare and condition your flowers, use a hand spray filled with water to refresh or revive them. Mist the flower heads from a distance of 8in (20cm) or so; don't get too close, or you may drench the petals and spoil them. Flowers such as hydrangeas particularly benefit from misting. A hand spray is also vital for misting floral foam arrangements, bouquets, and boutonnieres, as the stems will be out of water for a long period.

RECUTTING STEMS

Trim the stems with an angled cut 1–2in (2.5–5cm) at the end, depending on how long your stems are to begin with. If the flowers and foliage have woody stems, re-split the stems after you have trimmed them (p33). Then change the water and replace the flowers. If you have used an opaque vase, you can maintain the height of the original arrangement by packing a piece of cellophane or something similar into the base of the vase before you replace the flowers.

Trim all the stems by cutting them at an angle with florist's scissors.

INSIDER TIPS

• Bacteria can build up in water-filled vases, particularly in the corners, which can kill the flowers. Clean your vases thoroughly after each use with hot water, dishwashing liquid, and a bottle brush to scrub the edges of the vase well.

• Keep arrangements out of direct sunlight and away from radiators to prolong their life.

• If the moss discolors, put it in a sink and pour a kettle of boiling water over it to revive it.

CLEANING A VASE
Use a bottle brush to clean your vases and containers thoroughly every time you finish using them. This type of brush can be angled easily into awkward corners to lift out dirt and bacteria.

REVIVING FLOWERS

Lay floppy amaryllis or delphiniums on a table, prop up the stem ends so they tilt upward, fill the stems with water and leave for an hour or so until the stems are more rigid. The wilting petals of hydrangea are tough enough to survive being submerged in water for a minimum of two hours, or overnight, to revive them. To straighten and strengthen floppy gerberas, trim the stems, wrap them in newspaper, and leave in a vase of water for a few hours.

SPLIT STEMS

The fleshy stems of flowers such as amaryllis, hyacinths, and calla lilies can begin to look unsightly in a clear glass vase or container of water if they split. To prevent this happening, wrap a length of clear tape two or three times around the base of each stem after you have conditioned the flowers. This will ensure that the stems remain neat and won't splay. Then place the flower stems in the arrangement as usual.

Wrap gerbera stems in newspaper up to their necks, stand in a vase of water, and allow the newspaper to soak up the water and draw it up the lengths of the stems.

Gerberas absorb water both through the base of the stem and by osmosis through the surface area of the stem along its length.

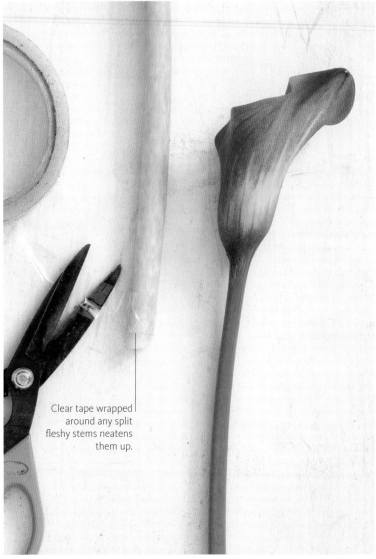

Clear tape wrapped around any split fleshy stems neatens them up.

FRONT-FACING VASE ARRANGEMENT

This step-by-step sequence explains how to arrange a vase of flowers in a simple but effective front-facing design. These straightforward steps will equip you with all the essential knowledge and skills you need to create any vase arrangement.

Before you arrange your flowers and foliage, cut the stems at an angle (keeping all the stems as long as possible until you arrange them), split any woody stems, take the pollen out of lilies, if using, and give them all a long drink in deep water (p33).

Basic materials

Flared vase
Sterilizing tablet or flower food
  (if using a clear glass vase)
Chicken wire (optional if using
  an opaque vase)
Florist's scissors

1 Fill a clean, well-washed, flared vase with fresh water and, if you are using a clear glass vase, add a sterilizing tablet. Arrange all the flowers and foliage into separate piles. Ideally, you want to have 5–8 stems each of two different types of foliage and 3–5 stems each of four different types of flower.

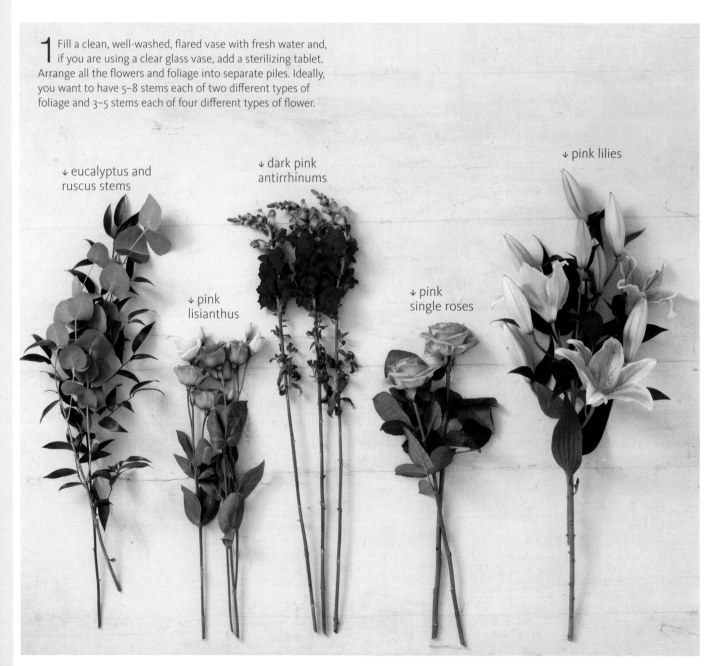

↓ eucalyptus and ruscus stems

↓ dark pink antirrhinums

↓ pink lilies

↓ pink lisianthus

↓ pink single roses

SKILLS

2 Place 3–4 stems of one type of foliage in the vase. These stems will naturally fall at an angle against the sides of the vase, creating a loose fan shape, and form a basic framework. They are designed to be slightly shorter than the other foliage. If you use an opaque vase, insert chicken wire into the vase first to ensure that each stem rests at the correct angle (right).

3 Add the second type of foliage in between the first stems. Stand each stem in front of the vase first to compare it to the display and gauge how much to trim it. Then cut and split it again and add it to the arrangement at an angle. If it still looks too tall, recut it and arrange it again. Shorter stems of foliage should stand at the front of the vase, with longer stems at the back and sides.

4 Once you have built up a good basic, but still quite sparse, fan shape, stop adding any more foliage for now.

5 Add the first variety of flower—usually those with the largest flower heads. Hold each flower stem at an angle in front of the vase where you think you would like to place it, then trim the end of the stem and insert it at an angle. At least one of these stems should be taller than the rest and stand at the back of the arrangement; stems placed at the front of the vase should be shortest.

6 Add the next variety of flower, angling each stem in front of the vase first to check its placing and height, and then inserting it at an angle. Although you need to judge the length of each stem individually, the aim is to create a graduated shape that is low at the front and tall at the back.

7 Turn the vase around so that you can view the display from the side and check on its graduated shape. If you use a clear vase, it's also worth glancing at the stems inside the vase at this point to check that they are positioned at an angle, which shows that you are building up the design in the correct way.

8 Add the third variety of flower, checking the height and position of each flower before you add it to the design. Place these flowers evenly through the design where there are gaps.

9 Insert the stems of the last type of flower in the same way. Using four varieties of flower in a vase arrangement ensures a rich texture and range of color, and creates more movement through the arrangement.

10 Add small stems of foliage at the edges and front to hide the top of the vase. As these stems are shorter, ensure that they sit in water; top up the vase if necessary once you have positioned it. Change the water every few days and recut the stems (if you have used chicken wire, lift the whole arrangement, with the chicken wire intact, out of the vase, trim the stems, and replace it in fresh water).

HAND-TIED BOUQUET

Our aim when making up a hand-tied bouquet is to keep the look of the bouquet quite compact, develop a rounded, or domed, shape with the flowers and foliage, and create a spiral effect with the stems. These are all aesthetic details that define our signature style.

Arranging a hand-tied bouquet is a methodical process. If you add your groups of flowers in the same sequence and turn the bunch slightly in the same direction every time you add a flower or a foliage stem, you should ensure that you won't place the same flowers next to each other as the bunch builds up. The binding point governs the size of a bouquet: if you hold the stems lower down, the arrangement will be looser, and the stems longer. A slightly higher binding point—holding the bunch of flowers about halfway to two-thirds of the way up their stems—will create the compact bouquet we prefer.

Basic materials

Florist's scissors
Raffia or garden string

1 Choose 3–6 stems each of five different flower varieties and 15 stems of foliage such as salal, and then condition them (p33).

← pink celosias

↓ astrantia

↓ pale pink single roses

↓ dark pink calla lilies

mauve → tracheliums

2 Arrange the flowers into individual piles so you can clearly see the colors and sizes of the different flower heads.

3 Choose a focal flower for the center of the bouquet. It should be something that is fairly big. In this case, a pink rose is a perfect choice. Add 3–4 stems of foliage in a circle around this first flower. The flower should sit just beneath the tips of the leaves. Hold the bunch at the binding point with your left hand if you are right-handed, and vice-versa if you are left-handed.

4 Pick another variety of flower and insert it into the bunch at the point where your thumb rests. Insert the stem at an angle so the end of the stem points toward your body and the flower head is angled away from you.

5 Place one of each of the other flowers around the foliage, turning the bunch slightly in the same direction after you have added each bloom. The flowers should, like the first rose, sit slightly lower than the tips of the foliage leaves.

6 Roughly trim the longer stems if the bunch becomes top-heavy. Don't cut the stems too short; you will need to trim all the stems properly later on. Add another circle of foliage at an angle, turning the bunch slightly as you work. The spiral of stems should now be apparent.

7 Look at the top of the bunch to check the position of the flowers and the balance of colors. Arrange the next sequence of flowers slightly lower around the sides to begin forming the domed shape. Use up the remaining flowers and foliage, angling these stems so that they sit even lower around the edges of the bunch.

8 Wrap a length of raffia or garden string a few times around the top of the binding point—immediately above your hand—and tie the ends firmly in a knot to secure the bunch. Trim off any excess raffia.

9 Trim the ends of the stems straight across so that the bunch can stand upright in a vase and all the stems will be in water. Re-split any woody stems.

10 A well-arranged, securely-tied bouquet like this should be able to stand upright unaided, as the spiral stems give it stability. Place the bouquet in a vase or, if it is a gift for someone, keep it in fresh, cool water until you are ready to wrap it and tie it with a ribbon (pp52–55), and then present it.

FLORAL FOAM ARRANGEMENT

A floral foam display is ideal if you want to create a low, compact design or a defined shape on a larger scale. Each flower and foliage stem is inserted at an angle to create the rounded or graduated contour that is so characteristic of these arrangements.

Floral foam must be soaked before you trim it, position it, and then arrange the flowers and foliage. Drop a block of floral foam into a bowl or bucket of water and lift it out as soon as it appears to have completely absorbed water or sunk to the bottom of the bucket; don't leave it in the water or it will begin to disintegrate. It's also worth using a hand spray regularly while you work to refresh the flowers.

Basic materials

Floral foam
Shallow bowl
Craft knife
Stem tape
Florist's scissors

1 Use 6–8 stems each of two different types of foliage, 7–11 stems each of three varieties of flower (or 2–3 stems if using spray flowers) for this small arrangement. Condition your flowers and foliage (p33). The stems will be cut quite short when you arrange them, so they don't need to be left too long when you condition them.

↓ purple veronica

white → lisianthus

eucalyptus → stems

↑ salal stems

↑ white single roses

2 Place half a block of soaked floral foam in the shallow bowl, trim the corners of the foam with a craft knife, and bind it to the bowl with stem tape.

3 Trim the smaller stems from the different sprays of foliage and use one variety of foliage to create a skeleton framework: insert a stem at an angle in each side of the foam at the base (so the leaves are angled downward to hide the base of the bowl), and three stems in a line across the top of the foam. Press the stems firmly, but not too far, into the foam—about ¾in (2cm) deep.

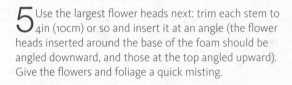

4 Add a few stems of the second type of foliage at an angle to fill the natural spaces in the foam. You want to achieve an even, rounded shape with the angled leaves, but not all the foam should be hidden at this stage.

5 Use the largest flower heads next: trim each stem to 4in (10cm) or so and insert it at an angle (the flower heads inserted around the base of the foam should be angled downward, and those at the top angled upward). Give the flowers and foliage a quick misting.

6 Insert the flowers evenly around the arrangement. Move the arrangement around as you work so that you distribute the flowers evenly. Here, four flowers have been inserted around the lower part of the foam, and three around the upper part.

7 Add a smaller flower next; spire-shaped flowers work well in an arrangement like this. Insert them at an angle in between the first flowers. Allow these spiky flowers to rise up out of the arrangement slightly to break the rounded contours of the other blooms.

9 Turn the arrangement around one last time to check for any gaps or visible foam, and fill or cover them with a stem of foliage.

8 If you use a variety of spray-shaped flower, cut off the shorter stems to use as individual blooms. Insert them into any obvious gaps in the arrangement.

10 Give the flowers and foliage a good misting with a hand mister. Before putting the display in position, tilt it over a kitchen sink to allow excess water to drain away, then dry the base of the container (this is especially important if you intend to hang a floral foam display as a pew end, for example). To prolong the life of the flowers, the foam must be kept moist: every 3–4 days, sit the arrangement on the draining board of the kitchen sink and gently pour a jug of water over it. Then mist the flowers and foliage again.

WIRED BOUTONNIERE

The point of wiring a single, beautiful flower in perfect condition is so that the flower head and any leaves surrounding it can be gently manipulated into the perfect angles once the boutonniere has been attached to the lapel of a jacket.

Fine wires and green stem tape are used to replicate the slim, smooth flower stem. The tape also seals in moisture to help the flower stay fresher for a little longer. It's important to keep the lengths of wire as straight as possible to avoid creating a bumpy effect that would look unsightly against the lapel of a suit.

Basic materials

Florist's scissors
Silver rose wires
Stem tape
22 gauge wire
Pearl pin

1 Choose three immaculate ivy leaves that will be large enough to cup the head of the rose. Turn one leaf over and insert a rose wire through either side of the spine (or midrib), making as small a stitch through the front as possible so the wire can't easily be seen.

2 Bend each side of the wire at 90° so the two lengths are parallel to the stem. Then twist one of the wires around both the stem and the remaining straight wire (this is known as a double leg mount).

3 Split a long length of stem tape in half with scissors (this is easily done by running the slightly open blades of the scissors up the center of the length of tape). Using thinner stem tape ensures a finer and more delicate result.

4 Attach one end of the thin stem tape to the top of the leaf stem. Wind the tape around and down the stem and wires, keeping the tape taut and stretching it as you wind it. Wind the tape down to the ends of the wires and back up again slightly. Pull off the excess tape with your fingers and seal it down. Repeat the process with the other two leaves.

5 To prepare the rose, bunch several rose wires together and fold them over the scissor blades at one end to create a small "U" shape in each wire. Snip off these folded ends to make staples. Press these staples into the sepals—the small green leaves immediately below the petals—so they are held in place.

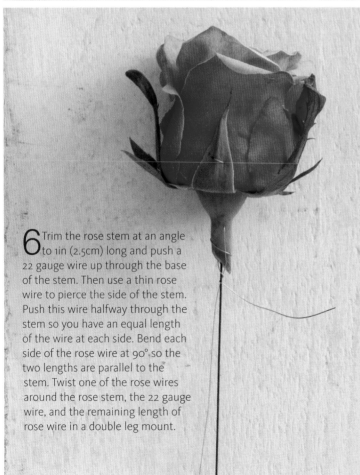

6 Trim the rose stem at an angle to 1in (2.5cm) long and push a 22 gauge wire up through the base of the stem. Then use a thin rose wire to pierce the side of the stem. Push this wire halfway through the stem so you have an equal length of the wire at each side. Bend each side of the rose wire at 90° so the two lengths are parallel to the stem. Twist one of the rose wires around the rose stem, the 22 gauge wire, and the remaining length of rose wire in a double leg mount.

7 Wind another length of thinned stem tape around the stem of the rose and the wires. Wrap the tape down to the ends of the wires and back up again slightly. Pull off the excess tape with your fingers and seal it down cleanly.

8 Place one of the wired leaves against the side of the rose so that the top of the leaf stem aligns with the top of the flower stem. Wrap only the wires together with stem tape so the stems themselves remain separated.

9 Bind the other two leaves to the flower in the same way, ensuring they are evenly spaced. Don't cut the length of florist's tape off when you attach the last leaf; you will need it shortly.

10 Trim the three leaf wires to different lengths to create a graduated effect. This means that as you push them against the 22 gauge wire they align smoothly and don't create a lumpy effect. Then cut the 22 gauge wire down to about 3in (8cm).

11 Wrap the loose end of the stem tape around the trimmed, graduated wires and down around the rose wire. Twist the tape around the base of the 22 gauge wire and then wind it back up the wire a little.

12 Massage the bound stem tape slightly in your fingers to seal it properly and then pull or cut off any excess tape. The wired stems should look and feel like one smooth flower stem.

13 To attach the wired rose to a jacket with a buttonhole, insert the wired stem through the buttonhole, and thread a pin through the underside of the lapel and around the stem to secure the rose in place.

14 Viewed from the front, only the rose and leaves are visible; gently tweak the leaves and flower head to show them off at their best angle.

ALTERNATIVE If a jacket has no buttonhole, place the wired rose against the front of a lapel, insert a pearl pin through the material, over the wired stem, and through the material again to secure the flower.

TYING

If you want to give flowers to someone as a gift, a few professional touches such as tying the arrangement skilfully can make all the difference between a sophisticated hand-tied bouquet and a rather loose, floppy bunch of flowers.

Even if you have bought a simple bunch of flowers, it's still worth unwrapping the bunch, rearranging the blooms, and re-tying them neatly so that they look their best.

The best materials to bind a bouquet are seagrass, raffia, and garden string. If you want to use a ribbon, secure the bunch at the binding point first and then tie the ribbon around the flower stems.

1 Lay the flowers and foliage on a bench or table and arrange them into a loosely spiralled bunch. You can, if you prefer, arrange them as a hand-tied bouquet in your hand (pp40–43).

2 Wrap a long length of seagrass (or raffia or garden string) twice around the stems at the binding point (just above your hand).

3 Bring the two ends of the raffia together and tie them together once. Then repeat the procedure with each end of seagrass to create a reef knot.

4 Pull the reef knot tight so it is secure and then trim the ends of the seagrass and the flower and foliage stems so they look neat.

WRAPPING

It's always best to wrap a hand-tied bouquet before you give it to someone as a gift: the wrapping paper helps to protect delicate petals in transit; and a well-wrapped bouquet makes a much more pleasing present.

Depending on the style, shape, and size of your bouquet and the colors of the flowers, choose a length of tasteful wrapping paper, cellophane, or simple brown paper, and select a ribbon that matches the predominant color of your bouquet.

1 Fold the wrapping paper in half at a slight angle (you may choose to have the pattern on the inside, as here). Place the bouquet of flowers on top of the paper so the binding point rests on the folded edge of the paper.

2 Fold one half of the wrapping paper carefully over the front of the flowers so the folded edge of the paper aligns with the outer edge of the bouquet.

3 Roll the bouquet up inside the rest of the paper, or fold the other half of the paper over the bouquet—whichever feels easier. Once the flowers are enclosed in the cone shape created by the paper, seal both sides of paper together with a small piece of clear tape.

4 To attach a ribbon around the base of the cone, you may need to pinch the folded paper together slightly first. Then wrap the ribbon twice around the stems and the base of the paper and secure the ends in a large bow. To prevent the bow looking lopsided, take the loops up rather than down as you tie them.

APPLY THE SKILLS

Now that you have learnt the basic techniques for creating a simple vase arrangement, a hand-tied bouquet, a floral foam display, and a wired flower (illustrated on pages 36–51), you can create all the designs shown here.

You also have all the essential knowledge you need to create the other arrangements in this book, each of which uses one of these basic techniques as a starting point.

VASE ARRANGEMENTS
Although these arrangements all vary in their style and appearance, and each display looks distinctly unique, they all contain the basic elements of a vase arrangement and are made up in much the same way.

SUNFLOWER VASE pp156–57

HAND-TIED BOUQUETS
With their precisely arranged blooms and impressive spiral stems, hand-tied arrangements make captivating gifts and bridal bouquets. These hand-tied bouquets have all been adapted slightly according to the season and the occasion.

SUMMER BOUQUET pp124–25

WINTER BRIDAL BOUQUET p201

COUNTRY SUMMER BRIDAL BOUQUET p131

DELPHINIUMS AND HYDRANGEAS IN BLUE pp144–45

ROSE AND LILAC URN pp104–105

FOLIAGE AND SEED HEAD DISPLAY pp146–49

SPRING BRIDAL BOUQUET p93

AUTUMN BOUQUET pp160–61

GREEN BOUQUET pp236–37

WINTER BOUQUET pp198–99

AUTUMN BRIDAL BOUQUET p177

SPRING BOUQUET pp82–83

FLORAL FOAM

The benefit of floral foam is that it is such an adaptable material to work with and, in turn, allows for a wide range of creative flower designs. The soaked floral foam can hold flowers and foliage at precise angles, which makes it ideal for modern, sculptural, and unusually shaped designs, as well as classic long and low, all-round, and front-facing foam arrangements.

COUNTRY SUMMER WEDDING PEW END pp132–33

SPRING WEDDING TABLE CENTERPIECE pp96–97

WIRED

Precise work is required to wire flowers and foliage, but the results are always exquisite. This selection of wired boutonniere, circlet, and vase arrangement shows how varied and useful the technique can be.

URBAN CHIC SUMMER WEDDING BOUTONNIERE p151

WALLPAPER ORCHIDS pp240–41

AUTUMN WEDDING BOUTONNIERE p177

SUMMER LONG AND LOW pp114–17

FLAG IRISES WITH HORSECHESTNUT pp98–99

SUMMER HARMONY pp112–13

COUNTRY SUMMER WEDDING TABLE CENTERPIECE
pp134–35

CREAM BASKET pp120–21

CARNATION SCULPTURE pp246–47

WINTER WEDDING BOUTONNIERE p201

ROSEBUD CIRCLET pp220–23

COUNTRY SUMMER WEDDING BOUTONNIERE p131

SECTION TWO
THROUGH THE YEAR

Seasonal flowers and foliage look their best when they are bought or picked in season, and they last longer. These arrangements give you an idea of the wonderful variety of flowers available through the year, and how you can use them.

HYACINTHS IN A PUSSY WILLOW FRAME

The catkin-covered willow frame in this appealing potted display supports a mass of hyacinth flower heads as they open and grow heavy on their stems. Buy the bulbs while they are still closed and arrange them in a cake pan or any round container. This display looks lovely on a kitchen or dining room table, or a low coffee table, and should last about three weeks if you mist the hyacinths every other day.

HOW TO ARRANGE

1 Line the cake pan with a piece of cellophane, trash bag, foil, or any other non-porous material to protect it.

2 Fill the pan almost to the top with potting soil.

3 Arrange the bulbs on the soil and fill the gaps around them with extra soil. Leave the tops of the bulbs uncovered, as this adds to the design.

4 Trim the ends (not the tips) of the pussy willow stems so that they are all roughly the same length (about 16in/40cm), and push the ends into the soil at regular intervals around the edge of the pan.

5 Guide each willow stem into the center with your hands and tie them together with a length of string or ribbon in a loose knot (see below).

6 Arrange some moss around the edge of the pan and over the soil to hide it, and then mist the hyacinth bulbs with water.

RIBBON TIE
If you have a length of ribbon that matches the color of the cake pan or hyacinth bulbs, use it to secure the willow stems together.

Flowers and foliage

↓ 7–11 hyacinth bulbs

2 bunches → pussy willow stems

↑ moss

Other materials

Cake pan (12in/30cm in diameter) or any round container
Cellophane, trash bag, foil (or any non-porous material)
Good-quality, multi-purpose potting soil
Shears
String or ribbon

Possible substitutions

'Tête à Tête' narcissi, grape hyacinths, or any other bulbs (for hyacinth bulbs); dogwood stems (for pussy willow stems)

SUSPENDED BULBS

This dogwood stem frame is designed to adapt to the individual sizes of hyacinth bulbs so they remain securely upright and don't topple over. (Hyacinth and amaryllis bulbs are the only spring bulbs heavy enough to work successfully in this vase design). If you top up the vase with water occasionally so the roots remain floating beneath the surface, this living room or bathroom arrangement will last for three weeks.

HOW TO ARRANGE

1 Trim the side shoots from the dogwood stems and cut the stems into equal lengths that are each a little longer than the width of the vase.

2 To make the frame, arrange three stems in a row on a flat surface. If any stems are very thin, reinforce them with an extra stem. Check that they are evenly spaced, and that together they are no wider than the width of the vase. Place another three stems over them at right angles to make a crosshatch effect. You should have four square spaces within the surrounds of the frame. Secure each cross-over point with string tied in a knot (see below, left).

3 Fill a third of the vase with pebbles, then fill the vase to the top with water.

4 Place the frame on the vase and position a bulb in a square hole. Adjust the frame around the bulb so it pinches the base of the bulb to secure it in place. Position the other bulbs in the same way on the frame.

ADJUSTABLE FRAME
String tied around the stems at each cross-over point enables each stem to be moved slightly.

FLOATING ROOTS
Only the roots of the bulbs need to float in the water to keep the hyacinths alive.

Flowers and foliage

↑ 4 hyacinth bulbs with soil washed off

3 dogwood → stems

Other materials

Clear cube vase (5½ x 5½in/ 14 x 14cm)
Pruning shears
String
Black pebbles or gravel

Possible substitutions

Amaryllis bulbs (for hyacinth bulbs); bamboo (for dogwood stems)

TULIPS IN A BOWL

This beautiful vase arrangement of long-stemmed French parrot tulips requires only a few flowers and grasses to create an arresting impact. The curved glass refracts the light and alters the hues to create a slightly softer effect when viewed from different angles. We have chosen French parrot tulips for their larger heads and extravagant petals with fluttery edges, and bear grass for its pliable properties, but you can use any tulips. This design makes a stylish display in a bathroom or as a table centerpiece at a dinner party in contemporary surroundings, and should last for a week if you keep them in good condition (pp34–35).

HOW TO ARRANGE

1 Fill the bowl with 2–2½in (5–6cm) water and add a sterilizing tablet.

2 Separate the grasses into two smaller bunches of about 10 stems each. Place the ends of one bunch in the water and loop the lengths around inside the bowl so they rise up and fall in a circular swirl.

3 Turn the bowl about a third of the way around, add the second bunch of grass, and create the same swirling effect.

4 Trim the ends of the tulips and take off any leaves that might touch or sit in the water. Bend each stem gently to arrange it inside the bowl; if it feels as if it will snap, gently massage the stem with your thumb and forefinger, moving from the base to the tip so that the flower droops towards the floor. Arrange the stem in between the grasses so that the flower head rests about two-thirds of the way up the side of the bowl. Arrange the rest of the tulips in a similar way to create a loose, slightly random, all-around arrangement of blooms.

INSIDER TIPS

- **French parrot tulips** tend to collect sand at the base of their bottom leaf where it joins the stem. Rinse this sand or grit off under running water before you arrange the flowers to prevent it spoiling the clear water.

- **Tulips continue to grow** after they have been cut, about 1in (2.5cm) a night if left in water, so it's worth positioning the flower heads a little lower in the vase to compensate for this extra growth.

Flowers and foliage

↓ 7–9 French parrot tulips

← 1 bunch bear grass

Other materials

Fishbowl (10in/25.5cm high)
Sterilizing tablet or flower food
Florist's scissors

Possible substitutions

Calla lilies or Singapore orchids (for French parrot tulips);
China grass (for bear grass)

TULIPS IN CUPS

Depending on the occasion or surroundings, the greatest impact can sometimes be made with the simplest of displays. This small, informal collection of plain cups and loosely arranged tulips is perfect for a dressing table, kitchen dresser, as individual place settings, or positioned in a row along a shelf or a table at a children's tea party. Choose tulip colors that suit the surroundings and limit yourself to a maximum of two colors; tulips that are the same color, or which harmonize or complement each other, make a stronger visual statement. They will last for a week if you keep them in good condition (pp34–35).

HOW TO ARRANGE

1 Clean the cups thoroughly and fill them two-thirds full of water.

2 Loosely arrange four yellow and four orange tulip stems in one hand. Strip off any leaves that might end up sitting in the water and trim the ends of the stems so that the flower heads will sit just above the rim of each cup.

3 Place the stems in a cup and adjust them so that they fall naturally in a random and informal way. The straight sides of the cups will make the tulips easier to arrange. Repeat the same process for the two remaining cup arrangements. Then top up the water to just below the rim of each cup.

INSIDER TIP

• **This arrangement works best** with a minimum of three cups of tulips, but make up as few or as many of these arrangements as you like to suit the space you have available and to create the right effect.

Flowers

← 4 yellow tulips per cup

← 4 orange tulips per cup

Other materials

3 straight-sided plain cups (4 x3in/10 x 7cm) or any simply colored or plain cups or teacups
Florist's scissors

Possible substitutions

Ranunculas, mixed narcissi, or daffodils

GELATIN MOLD MIX

An abundance of blooms are packed into an old-fashioned ceramic gelatin mold to create this luscious all-around vase display. This is a very full arrangement; whatever size mold you use, be aware that the larger the mold, the more flowers you will need. It will look charming in a conservatory or a country kitchen, or as a lightly scented table centerpiece for a dinner table. It should last about five days (pp34–35).

HOW TO ARRANGE

1 Arrange a piece of chicken wire inside the mold (p37). Don't scrunch the wire up too much or the hyacinth stems won't fit through the holes. Fill about two-thirds of the mold with water.

2 If you can't find four varieties of flowers, use three varieties instead and use more of them. Arrange the hyacinths first, as they are the biggest blooms and will provide some support for the other flowers. Insert one or two through the center of the chicken wire and place the rest around the edges of the bowl.

3 Bluebells, tulips, and grape hyacinths look better if they are grouped in small bunches. Fill in the gaps in the chicken wire around the hyacinths from the center outward with a few stems of each flower so that they are massed together as injections of color that lead your eye around the arrangement.

GELATIN MOLDS
Use gelatin molds in various sizes for different occasions. Miniature gelatin molds, for example, can be used for individual place settings.

Flowers

30 bluebells →

5 pink hyacinths ↓

↓ 25 pink tulips

30 grape hyacinths →

Other materials

Oblong gelatin mold, pie dish, or modern stainless steel mold (8in/20cm in diameter)
Chicken wire
Florist's scissors

Possible substitutions

Ranunculus (for tulips); narcissi (for bluebells); freesias (for grape hyacinths)

WHITE CUBE

This tonal composition of creamy white flowers is arranged so that the individual blooms are bunched in four equal groups to create a checkerboard effect. Although this is intended to be a monochrome all-around vase arrangement, its clever design gradually draws your eye to the subtle differences in flower shapes and the hints of green and yellow that intersperse the white tones. Small-headed spray roses make a good substitute if you can't find one of these particular varieties of flower. The arrangement is best placed on a low coffee table so that the flowers can be seen from above, and it should last for a week if you keep the flowers in good condition (pp34–35).

HOW TO ARRANGE

1 Gather each variety of flower into a hand-tied bunch with the stems straight rather than spiraled: take two stems and add more flowers at an upright angle to them, turning the bunch around slightly in the same direction in your hand as you add to it. Each bunch must be roughly the same size, so use fewer hyacinth stems than you would narcissi, for example.

2 Tie each bunch at the binding point with a length of raffia.

3 Trim the stems of all the flowers to the same length.

4 Fill two-thirds of the vase with water and arrange the bunches of flowers so that they stand upright in the vase and overhang the edges slightly. There should be no gaps between the separate "squares" of flowers. Finally, top up the vase with water.

INSIDER TIPS

• **This design can be recreated** in any size; the smaller the container, the fewer flowers you will need, though use a minimum of five stems of each flower to achieve the same look.

• **You may need** to re-cut the tulip stems more often than the other flowers, as they will continue to grow after they have been arranged (p67).

Flowers

30 paper → white narcissi

↓ 25 white ranunculas

25 white single tulips ↓

↓ 15 white hyacinths

Other materials

White cube vase (7 x 7in/18 x 18cm)
Raffia
Florist's scissors

Possible substitutions

For a yellow design use: daffodils (for narcissi); yellow freesias (for tulips); yellow single roses (for hyacinths); yellow spray roses (for ranunculas)

NARCISSI BULBS AND DOGWOOD STEMS

A potted all-around arrangement like this situated on a kitchen table, windowsill, in a hallway, or even in a bathroom is a wonderful way to welcome the onset of spring and bring its vibrant, fresh colors indoors. The display may appear complicated, but is quite simple to arrange. A straight-sided rectangular glass vase is a crucial element of the design, as it dictates the visually striking, graphic look, but any spring bulbs will work well. The flowers should last for up to two weeks if you buy bulbs with their flowers still in bud, and always keep the compost slightly moist.

Flowers and foliage

↓ 3 small pots 'Tête à Tête' narcissi bulbs

↑ moss

2 bunches →
dogwood stems

HOW TO ARRANGE

1 Line the vase with a large square of cellophane (it doesn't need to be smooth and crease-free, as it will be completely hidden). Fill two-thirds of the vase with potting soil and press it down firmly. Take off any side shoots from the dogwood stems, trim the base of each stem so its end is flat, and push the stems in between the compost-filled cellophane and the side of the vase so that they butt up next to each other in a straight line. The pressure of the soil will hold them in place.

Other materials

Rectangular clear glass vase
 (7½in/19cm high,
 9½in/24cm long)
Cellophane
Good-quality, multi-purpose
 potting soil
Florist's scissors

Possible substitutions

Any bulbs in season (for
 narcissi bulbs); bamboo
 (for dogwood stems)

2 Use a pair of scissors to trim the dogwood stems down to the same level as the rim of the vase. Continue to place more stems in a line around the remaining sides of the vase and trim each of them down.

3 Check that the dogwood stems are all straight and butt right up to one another before you trim them across the top. Don't worry if the trimmed stems look a little uneven when you've cut them, as they can always be covered with moss at the end.

4 Remove the bulbs from their pots and arrange them on top of the soil. Fill the gaps around the bulbs with more soil and firm it down gently with your fingers. Moisten the flowers and soil with a misting of water.

5 Carefully cut the excess cellophane away with the scissors so that it can't be seen above the trimmed dogwood stems. Arrange moss over the soil so that it is completely hidden, and give the flowers another misting.

INSIDER TIPS

• **When you buy spring bulbs** in pots, avoid any pot-bound plants with roots that have spread out from the base of the pot, as they usually experience reduced growth. Look instead for plants with good green foliage and no brown or yellow leaf tips.

• **To get the maximum pleasure** from an arrangement like this, keep it in a cool room away from heat sources such as radiators and out of direct sunshine so that the buds open slowly and the flowers stay alive longer. An occasional misting of the flowers and soil—perhaps every two to three days—ensures that the display will remain in good condition for as long as possible.

SPRING FANTASY

This ebullient burst of spring color, energy, and growth has three components: an apple blossom tree (pp90–91), a vase arrangement (pp36–39) of vibrantly colored pink double hyacinths, tulips, and double red tulips, and individual hyacinth bulbs in their original pots. The apple blossom tree stands inside a wooden box, and packed around it are recycled plastic bags to build up the base so that the hyacinth bulbs and vase arrangement can be easily seen.

EFFECT Using terra-cotta pots and natural wood with bulbs and blossom conveys a sense of the garden coming to life in spring as gardeners dust off their tools in the potting shed.

SHAPE This is intended to be a large, open design with interesting details: under the arching scented branches of an apple tree, bulbs push their way through small mounds of moss that recreate a grass lawn.

COLOR Although yellow is the color most often associated with spring, we've chosen pink flowers to complement the tall branches of apple blossom at the back of the design.

NARCISSI TREE

The clean parallel lines of a ceramic vase echo the straight stems of narcissi in this tonally pleasing floral foam design. Its shapes and proportions are also exact: the stems and vase are the same height, and the slightly splayed stems, fixed in floral foam, are reflected in the gentle flare of the vase. This display looks stunning in a modern kitchen, on a hall table, or as one of a matching pair on a mantelpiece, and lasts up to a week if you keep the foam moist.

HOW TO ARRANGE

1 Narcissi stems are quite fragile, so carefully arrange them as a hand-tied bunch with straight (rather than spiralled) stems. Turn the bunch around slightly in the same direction every time you add a flower, and arrange the last stems a little lower around the edges of the bunch to give an all-around domed effect.

2 Tie the stems with a length of raffia wrapped just below the flower heads so it can't be seen (below left). Don't tie them too tight, or you could crush the stems. Trim the ends of the stems so that they are all the same length.

3 Pack a piece of cellophane or similar material into the base of the vase to give the stems added height. Place the bunch in the vase and wedge squares of soaked floral foam around the stems to support them so they stand upright. The top of the foam should sit 1in (2.5cm) below the rim of the vase. Fill the vase almost to the top with water and cover the top of the foam with a layer of shells.

Flowers

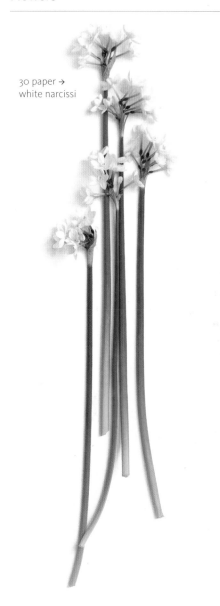

30 paper → white narcissi

HIDDEN BINDING POINT
This binding point is high to hide the raffia beneath the flower petals.

DECORATIVE SHELLS
Shells are an attractive way to cover unsightly floral foam.

Other materials

Ceramic flared vase (10in/25cm high)
Florist's scissors
Raffia
Cellophane
Floral foam
Decorative shells, gravel, sand, or colored glass

Possible substitution

Daffodils

SPRING BOUQUET

This hand-tied bouquet of vibrant flowers is made up of contrasting blues and oranges that enhance each other so that the blooms sing with intensity. If you use hyacinths and grape hyacinths from your garden, cut the stems as long as possible; if they are much shorter than the other stems, reduce the number of flowers and cut their stems shorter to make a posy. If grape hyacinths are hard to find, try using lilac freesia instead. This bouquet looks sensational in an orange or black glass vase as a table centerpiece, or it could make a gorgeous gift for a birthday or for Mother's Day. It should last at least a week (pp34–35).

HOW TO ARRANGE

1 Divide the different flower varieties into separate piles. Hold a hyacinth in your hand at the binding point. This bouquet is compact, so keep the binding point just higher than halfway up the stem. Add another flower at an angle, twisting the bunch around slightly in one direction in your hand as you do so.

2 Add a stem of salal and one of each of the flower varieties (add the grape hyacinths in groups of three for a better effect). Recess the tulips slightly, as they will continue to grow. Check that you are happy with the arrangement, then add more stems at the same angle to create a spiral stem effect. Keep turning the bunch around slightly in the same direction as you work.

3 Arrange the last layer of flowers a little lower around the edges to give a slightly domed look.

4 Tie the bunch at the binding point with a length of raffia or garden string and secure in a knot.

5 Cut the stems at an angle so they are roughly the same length and will all be able to sit in water. If you are giving the bouquet as a gift, stand it in fresh water until you need it, then wrap it in paper and tie it with a ribbon (pp54–55) to present it.

Flowers and foliage

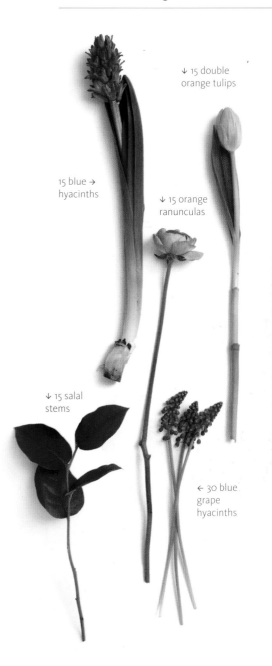

↓ 15 double orange tulips

15 blue → hyacinths

↓ 15 orange ranunculas

↓ 15 salal stems

← 30 blue grape hyacinths

Other materials

Florist's scissors
Raffia or garden string

Possible substitutions

Lilac freesias (for grape hyacinths); ruscus or variegated pittosporum (for salal)

CONTRASTING COLORS
Although these orange and blue (or purple) flowers vary in color and tone, they enhance each other when massed together. This is because they sit opposite each other on the color wheel.

FLOATING RANUNCULAS

The simple, restrained style of this vase arrangement captures the essence and intricacy of nature in a distilled form, although the slightly random stem lengths of the ranunculas give it a touch of lively informality. A rectangular or cube glass vase is best for this design because it automatically imposes an element of uniformity and order, but a small fishbowl would make an attractive alternative. This concise, considered arrangement will provide a stylish focal point in your bedroom, living room, or kitchen, or on a dining table. It will last for a week if you keep the flowers in good condition (pp34–35).

Flowers

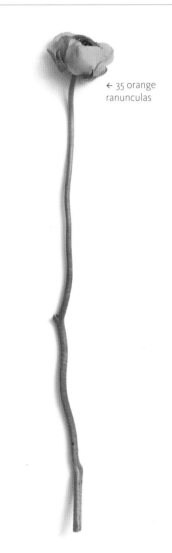

← 35 orange ranunculas

HOW TO ARRANGE

1 Half-fill the vase with water and add a sterilizing tablet. To make a grid over the vase, place strips of tape about ½in (1.5cm) apart across its length and its width. The square holes created by this grid should neither be too small to insert the stems nor so large that the flowers fall through.

Other materials

Rectangular glass vase
  (7½in/19cm high,
  9½in/24cm long)
Sterilizing tablet or flower food
Tape
Florist's scissors
Craft knife

Possible substitutions

White roses, or white or yellow
  Icelandic poppies

2 Press the tape down onto the edges of the vase to secure it properly, and trim off the excess tape with a craft knife so the grid appears invisible.

INSIDER TIP

• **Ranunculas have many smaller buds** that grow on short stalks along the length of their main stem. Recycle these offshoots by gathering them into an informal bunch, trimming the ends of the stems to the same length, and arranging them in a small square glass vase that you can place near the main arrangement for added interest.

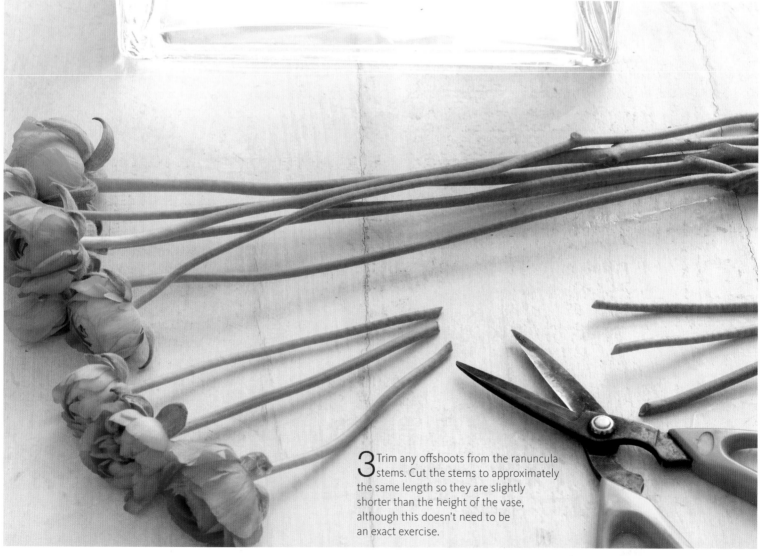

3 Trim any offshoots from the ranuncula stems. Cut the stems to approximately the same length so they are slightly shorter than the height of the vase, although this doesn't need to be an exact exercise.

4 Depending on the size of the flower heads, place one or two ranunculas in each square hole.

5 When you have placed all the flowers in the square holes, check for any visible gaps and add an extra flower if necessary to hide the tape grid and give the illusion that the flowers are suspended in air. Check that the end of each stem sits in the water, and top up the vase with more water if needed.

CHERRY BLOSSOM TREE IN A VASE

The beauty of nature so delicately stylized in Japanese paintings is the inspiration for this stunning yet simple celebration of spring—an informal, front-facing vase arrangement that looks like a tree in blossom. There are no rules, so the aim is to make it look as natural as possible. Cherry blossom can be quite branched, so you only need a few branches with the blossom still in bud. It works well on the floor of a large, airy hall, white living room, porch, or lobby, and should last for a week (pp34–35). If you have any offcuts, arrange them in a small vase as a scaled-down version of the display.

HOW TO ARRANGE

1 Treat the branches like woody-stemmed flowers: cut and split the stems (p32) and leave them in a bucket of water for an hour before arranging them.

2 Completely cover a heavy-based column vase in strips of bark bought from sustainable sources or a good florist. Bind the bark to the vase with lengths of seagrass secured in a knot. Fill the vase with water.

3 Recut and split the stems, taking off about 1in (2.5cm); the more water these branches can draw up, the longer they last. The lengths of the stems should be two or three times the height of the vase to keep the proportions correct.

4 Place one branch in the vase and let it fall naturally at an angle. Arrange another branch so it mirrors the shape of the first branch. Position a third branch in the center so that it leans forward slightly to give a three-dimensional effect.

5 Add a few slightly taller branches to balance out the arranged branches; you want to achieve a pleasing mix of branches, blossom, and air in between.

Flowers and casing

← 5 cherry blossom branches

← bark strips

NATURAL MATERIALS
Bark, a useful resource for covering containers and vases, has a wonderful textural quality, as does a natural cord such as seagrass.

Other materials

Column vase (24in/61cm high) or a galvanized garden bucket with chicken wire inside
Shears
Seagrass, rope, or garden string

Possible substitutions

Magnolia branches in bud (for cherry blossom branches); hessian (for bark strips)

SPRING WEDDING

With their cheerful, uplifting colors that carry the promise of bright days ahead, spring flowers are perfect for these classic, yet quite informal, wedding designs. Condition them really well before arranging them (pp32–33), and keep them misted or in water until the last minute (and dry the bouquet stems with a cloth so they don't spoil the bride's dress).

BOUTONNIERE
7 lily of the valley
3 lily of the valley leaves

BOUQUET
10 yellow freesias
10 cultivated guelder
7 cream spray roses
10 cream parrot tulips

PEW END
15 cream parrot tulips
15 cream tulips

TABLE CENTERPIECE
Selection of yellow spring flowers, such as fritillaria, tulips, freesias, and daffodils according to your personal preference, and flat and bun moss.

← lily of
the valley

← cultivated
guelder

← yellow
freesias

cream →
spray roses

← cream
tulips

← yellow
tulips

cream →
parrot
tulips

← flat moss

BOUTONNIERE

Sweetly scented, delicate lily of the valley flowers make an unusual but attractive choice for a boutonniere. This arrangement is simple to create, because the flower stems don't need to be wired.

1 Give the flowers a good drink of water the day before, then trim off any leaves and simply gather seven stems of lily of the valley together in a mini spiral of flowers.

2 Add a couple of the leaves around the back of the boutonniere, and fold a third leaf in half and place it at the front of the arrangement.

3 Secure the boutonniere with a length of raffia tied in a neat knot and supply it with a pearl-tipped pin to attach it onto the lapel of a jacket.

BOUQUET

This gorgeous cream, yellow, and green bouquet needs to be slightly more rounded and domed than a normal hand-tied bouquet.

1 Divide the different flowers into separate piles. Hold a flower stem in your hand and add another variety of flower to it. Twist the bunch around slightly in your hand as you do so.

2 Add more stems at the same angle to create a spiral stem effect. Keep turning the bunch in the same direction as you work. Add one of each of the different flowers until you have included all the blooms and have a balanced look. Recess the tulips slightly if you make the bouquet the day before it is needed.

3 Arrange the last two layers of flowers slightly lower around the edges for a domed effect.

4 Tie the bunch with a length of raffia or string. Cover the raffia with a long length of thick cream ribbon, wrapped several times around the stems, and tied in a knot. Trim the stem ends straight across with garden shears.

PEW END

As tulips continue to grow once cut, they can make an arrangement look slightly disordered overnight; it is best to arrange these blooms on the morning of the wedding.

1 Strip most of the leaves from the stems, leaving a few odd leaves for color and interest, and get rid of any drooping leaves. Arrange the tulip stems like a spiral bouquet (pp40–43), but make it up facing you and position the flowers at the back slightly higher.

2 Tie off the bunch with raffia or string.

3 Wrap a long length of strong wire a couple of times around the stems on top of the raffia. Tie the ends around the top of the pew to secure the bunch.

4 Cover the raffia/wire binding point with a length of cream ribbon tied in a bow.

TABLE CENTERPIECE

Once you have arranged your selection of flowers, position the
various containers in an informal circular or linear arrangement,
depending on the shape of the table. Make up
smaller arrangements of just three
containers or so for other tables.

1 Select the containers you want to use and line any non-watertight containers with a square of cellophane or part of a trash bag or plastic shopping bag.

2 Place a block of soaked floral foam in the center of each container. Trim the edges of any cellophane to the top of the container.

3 Arrange tulips and freesias in the foam: cut off lower leaves and offshoot buds (reserve these for a small vase display) and trim the stems. Press a stem into the center of the foam, then add more, working out from the center at a slight angle.

4 Cover the gaps between the flowers with flat moss. Arrange daffodils, fritillaria, and offshoot buds in clear glass vases and use bun moss on its own in the smallest pots.

FLAG IRISES WITH HORSECHESTNUT

Young flag irises gathered from the garden feature in this all-around spring arrangement in floral foam. Their stems have been cut short so they bloom beneath a canopy of horsechestnut leaves, and together they are reminiscent of the different scale and diversity of nature. Choose a thin, streamlined, opaque vase or container to create the right look for this design, and use half-opened buds and horsechestnut stems with their leaves just emerging and unfurling. Position the arrangement on a shelf or mantelpiece in a light, airy room for the maximum impact. The flowers should last for seven days if you keep them in good condition (pp34–35).

HOW TO ARRANGE

1 Soak two blocks of floral foam, then trim or cut them into pieces so that they fit snugly inside the vase.

2 Press a straight line of horsechestnut stems of varying heights into the foam along the center of the vase.

3 Cut the iris stems very short—to about 3in (8cm)—and tuck them into the foam in a line in front of and behind the horsechestnut stems so that the flower heads rise just above the neck of the vase. Put the vase in position and top it up with water.

INSIDER TIP

• **Horsechestnut stems last for several weeks**, so just keep replacing the irises as they start to fade. Change the water every few days by standing the vase on a draining board or in the kitchen sink and pouring in enough water so that the old, stale water is flushed out.

Flowers and foliage

← 30 flag irises

← 9 horsechestnut stems

Other materials

Thin, rectangular, opaque vase
  (3in/7.5cm deep,
  15½in/40cm long)
Floral foam
Florist's scissors

Possible substitutions

Standard irises, tulips, or daffodils (for flag irises); birch twigs or magnolia branches (for horsechestnut stems)

IRIS BOWL

This unadulterated display of purple irises is a striking yet delightful design that will liven up any coffee table or circular dining table. The binding point of the hand-tied bouquet is much lower than normal so that the tall iris stems and their intensely colored flower heads can flare out dramatically over the sides of the fishbowl. Green dogwood stems are fresh and quite pliable, so they are curled inside the bowl to give added definition to its curved contours. This all-around arrangement should last for a week (pp34–35).

HOW TO ARRANGE

1 Trim any offshoots from the dogwood stems.

2 Fill the fishbowl with 2–2½in (5–6cm) of water and add a sterilizing tablet.

3 Choose fresh dogwood that is sprouting, as the stems will be more malleable. Place the end of a stem in the water and curl the length of the stem up to the widest part of the bowl. Turn the bowl around slightly and arrange another stem, echoing the same curve as the first stem. Keep turning the bowl in the same direction and massage and add the rest of the stems in a linear pattern so that they don't look messy.

4 Arrange the irises in a hand-tied spiral bouquet with a low binding point, as the neck of the bowl will support the stems. Hold an iris in your hand and add another iris at an angle. Add more stems to create a spiral effect and keep turning the bouquet around in the same direction as you work. Arrange the last flowers a little lower around the edges to create a slightly domed effect.

5 Tie the bunch with a length of thick green aluminum wire (see below) and place it in the center of the bowl so that it stands upright.

Flowers and foliage

← up to 10 green dogwood stems

↓ 3 bunches long-stemmed irises

Other materials

Fishbowl (10in/25.5cm high)
Florist's scissors
Sterilizing tablet or flower food
Thick green aluminum wire

Possible substitutions

Gerbera or paper white narcissi (for irises); yellow weeping willow stems (for dogwood stems)

SECURE BINDING POINT
As the binding point is so low and the bunch is top-heavy, wrap the wire several times around the stems to hold them securely in place.

LILAC GARDEN PITCHER

The lush abundance of the countryside in the early months of summer is captured perfectly by this uncomplicated arrangement in a plain pitcher. The flowers are arranged as a spiral hand-tied bouquet without being tied off, which would make the blooms look too tight. Instead, they are placed straight in the pitcher to fall naturally in a loose arrangement, as if they have just been picked from the garden. Any other garden flowers would work equally well in this design, and it will look lovely set on a round table outside at a barbecue, or in the kitchen. It should last for five days (pp34–35).

HOW TO ARRANGE

1 Arrange the different flowers into separate piles (euphorbia and alchemilla are treated as flowers in this arrangement). Hold the stem of a flower in your hand and add another variety of flower to it at the binding point, twisting the bunch around slightly in one direction in your hand as you do so.

2 Add one of each of all the flowers alternately at the same angle to create a spiral stem effect, turning the bunch in the same direction as you work.

3 Check that you are happy with the arrangement, then add the remaining blooms and arrange the last layer of flowers at a more acute angle so the flower heads sit a little lower around the edges of the bunch and create a domed effect.

4 Holding the bunch in one hand, cut the stems at an angle so they are all the same length. Place the flowers in the pitcher and adjust them slightly if need be to make an all-around display. Fill almost to the brim with water.

Flowers

← 7 lilac stocks

↓ 6 alchemilla

↓ 5 spurge euphorbia

↓ 12 French lavender

7 ageratum →

← 5 lilac

Other materials

Enamel pitcher (8in/21cm high)
Florist's scissors

Possible substitutions

Antirrhinums (for stocks); spray roses (for ageratum); phlox (for lilac); marguerites (for French lavender); cultivated guelder (for euphorbia); eucalyptus (for alchemilla)

FOLIAGE AS FLOWERS
Some foliage, such as alchemilla, is such an attractive color and shape that it can be treated like a flower and feature in a display.

ROSE AND LILAC URN

This impressive front-facing vase arrangement appears to have an abundance of flowers in soft shapes and colors, although in fact much of the substance is created by carefully arranged foliage, which provides a strong visual framework in which to place the flowers. Its proportions aren't huge—the vase and flowers reach a height of 34in (87cm) or so, but you'll need a large, sturdy, watertight urn to balance the arrangement and create the right visual effect. This display will look as good in a simple, white, minimalist living room as it will in a grand entrance hall or as a table centerpiece at a dinner party. It should last up to seven days if you keep the flowers and foliage in good condition (pp34–35).

HOW TO ARRANGE

1 Line the glass urn with the monstera leaves and place a piece of chicken wire inside the rim. Fill two-thirds of the urn with water and add a sterilizing tablet.

2 Group the flowers and foliage into separate piles and build up a framework of foliage (p37) using the white leaf and viburnum stems.

3 Arrange those flowers with darker hues first, such as the alstroemeria and lilacs, so that you will know where best to place the more dominant pink roses and stocks. Place the lilacs around the sides and in the middle so they can hang attractively. Then add the roses and stocks. Turn the vase and check its profile as you work to ensure that you have a graduated front-facing shape. When you have added all the flowers and foliage, top the vase up with water.

Flowers and foliage

← 5 red alstroemeria

← 7 pale pink spray roses

↓ 6 cultivated guelder stems

5 lilac → stocks

6 dark → pink lilacs

3 white → leaf stems

5 garden viburnum stems →

← 2 monstera leaves

Other materials

Clear glass or opaque urn or flared vase (18in/46cm high)
Chicken wire
Sterilizing tablet or flower food
Florist's scissors

Possible substitutions

Lisianthus (for spray roses); antirrhinums (for stocks)

HIDDEN STEMS
Two monstera leaves line this clear vase to hide most of the stems. They also transform the urn into a lovely lush green color that sets off the flowers and foliage beautifully.

SUPPORTING ROLE
Foliage enhances flowers beautifully and shows them at their best. Mixed seasonal foliage, such as this cultivated guelder and garden viburnum, also provides visual interest in an arrangement.

ROSE TOPIARY TREE

The restrained elegance of this spray rose floral foam arrangement is due in large part to its limited ingredients—this is another example of a mass of just one variety of flower creating an eye-catching display. The proportions of the arrangement are designed so that the container is slightly taller than the twigs, and the twigs are a little longer than the rose ball. Floral foam balls are sold in various sizes, and although this display has been made with the smallest-sized foam ball available, it can be recreated on a much larger scale. This handsome design would look good on a desk in a study or a library, a hall table, or on a side table in a living room. It needs misting every other day to keep the blooms fresh, and should last four to five days.

HOW TO ARRANGE

1 Tie the bundle of birch twigs securely with a length of raffia about 4–5in (10–12cm) up from the base of the bundle. Tie the ends of the twigs with another length of raffia. Cut the branched tips of the birch twigs off just above the top raffia tie.

Flowers and foliage

← 1 bundle of birch twigs

← 15 'Mimi Eden' spray roses open and in bud

↓ moss

Other materials

Opaque urn (8in/20cm high)
Raffia
Florist's scissors
Cellophane
1 block floral foam
1 small floral foam ball

Possible substitutions

Spray carnations (for spray roses); bamboo (for birch twigs)

2 Line the urn with a square of cellophane if it is not watertight. Place a soaked square of floral foam, cut to fit, inside the urn.

3 Push the soaked foam ball onto the tied twigs, then push the base of the twigs into the square foam in the urn. Cut off the top raffia binding under the foam ball, but keep the lower binding in place.

4 Trim the stems of the buds and roses to 2in (5cm). Group two or three rose heads together and press them into the foam ball. Fill in the gaps around them with buds. Continue until the ball is covered.

INSIDER TIP

• **If you like the idea** of converting the rose ball into a hanging display (like a pomander), push a length of wire through the center of the ball after you've soaked it, wrap one end of the wire around a small, short twig to hold the wire securely in place, and fashion the other end into a loop to hang the ball up (p244). Cover the ball in roses or peonies and hang it from an overhanging branch near or above a table set for lunch in the garden.

• **Moss should last well** in an arrangement like this, particularly if you mist it with water when you spray the roses. If the moss begins to discolor, place it in a bowl, pour boiling water over it to revive it, and rearrange it over the floral foam.

5 Trim the cellophane so that it is level with the rim of the urn, then cover the square foam and cellophane with moss so that they are both hidden.

SUMMER HARMONY

A traditional front-facing arrangement such as this needs to be rigid and structured; it often looks better if it has an informal style that doesn't balance exactly. The randomly arranged purple hydrangeas and deep purple veronicas and campanula contrast beautifully with the pale roses and foxgloves. Set against a backdrop of wavy, rich-green forsythia foliage, they make a sumptuous-looking display that would look impressive in a tent for a party, in a large hallway, or in a church. The blooms will last for up to five days if you mist them often and keep the floral foam wet.

HOW TO ARRANGE

1 Trim the blocks of soaked foam and place them inside the container. Bind the foam and container together with florist's tape.

2 As this is a front-facing arrangement, place the tallest stems of forsythia into the top of the foam at the center back. Angle them so they tilt back slightly. Then place shorter stems at an upward-facing angle at each side of the foam (p45), and even shorter stems at the center front. Build up the remaining forsythia around this framework to create a loose, triangular shape.

3 Place the three hydrangea heads near the front of the arrangement, then add the single roses and spray roses. Together, these flowers should provide a balance of shape and color throughout the arrangement.

4 Arrange the foxgloves next, placing them in groups near the back of the arrangement to give extra height.

5 Place the campanula and veronica last, using them to fill any obvious gaps and balance out the color scheme.

Flowers and foliage

↓ 6 purple veronica

← 7 pale pink foxgloves

↓ 9 single pale pink roses

10 cultivated purple campanula →

← 3 pale pink spray roses

← 12 forsythia stems

↑ 3 aubergine hydrangeas

Other materials

Deep-sided round or square plastic bowl
2 blocks floral foam
Florist's tape
Craft knife
Florist's scissors

Possible substitutions

Delphiniums (for foxgloves), stocks (for veronica), peonies (for hydrangea), privet (for forsythia)

FLOWER SHAPES
This arrangement combines several different flower shapes in an effective way: large, soft domed shapes are balanced by tall spires and spears.

SUMMER LONG AND LOW

A long and low arrangement is not something that we do that often, but it has its place: this is a classic way to display beautiful fresh flowers in a traditional setting or at a formal dinner party. This design could work equally well placed on a low coffee table or at the center of a boardroom table in an office. The benefit of creating such a low-spreading arrangement is that everyone can see the flowers from above. If you mist the flowers every other day and keep the foam wet, it should last for four or five days.

Flowers and foliage

← 6 'Dauco Corato' dill

← 7 'Aqua' single roses

↓ 1 garden viburnum stem (cut down into small sprays with short stems)

↓ 7 pink spray roses

← 6 astrantia

6 alchemilla → (cut down into small sprays with short stems)

6 salal stems →

HOW TO ARRANGE

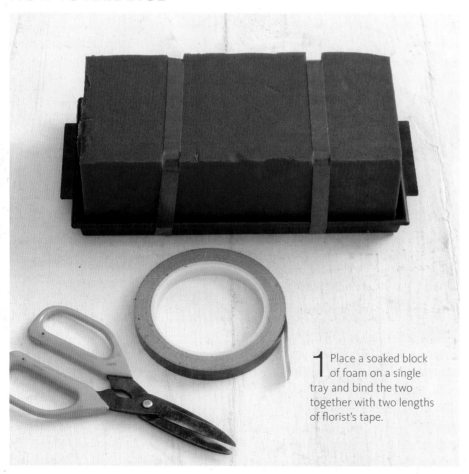

1 Place a soaked block of foam on a single tray and bind the two together with two lengths of florist's tape.

Other materials

Block of floral foam and single plastic tray
Florist's tape
Florist's scissors

Possible substitutions

Trachelium (for dill); freesias (for spray roses); peonies (for single roses)

2 Set the height, length, and width of the arrangement with the first few stems of viburnum. Press a stem in at an angle on each side of the foam and position three stems along the top to create a skeleton shape and spine.

3 Build up the basic shape by adding the salal and more stems of viburnum.

4 Place the stems of remaining foliage at similar angles to make a green framework of smooth contours within which to place the flowers.

5 Arrange the large pink single roses. Place the first rose in the middle to gauge the right height, then arrange the rest of the roses alternately on either side of the central spine and around the sides. Cut the stems to about 3–4in (7–10cm).

6 Place the deeper pink spray roses next, ensuring that you maintain an even visual balance with the larger roses and foliage.

7 Add the dark dill and astrantia blooms, filling in areas where there are still gaps.

8 Add the sprays of alchemilla last to fill any obvious gaps and balance out the shape and color of the arrangement. Add odd pieces of viburnum and salal if the foam still shows through.

SHAPE AND TEXTURE
Although both pink in color, these spiky little astrantia and smooth-petalled, velvety roses have been placed together to accentuate their diverse shapes and textures.

CREAM BASKET

The mix of delicate white flowers and cream roses in this all-around floral foam design are carefully chosen to match exactly the color of the oval enamel basket. Together they create a lovely light, fresh-looking centerpiece that is shown off to best effect on a long tressle table set for lunch or dinner in the backyard, or on a low table indoors. The arrangement will last up to seven days if you mist the flowers regularly to keep them fresh and ensure that the floral foam stays wet.

HOW TO ARRANGE

1 Place a block or two of soaked floral foam inside the basket. If your container isn't watertight, fix the block to a plastic tray before you put it in position. The foam should sit about 1in (2.5cm) above the rim of the container so that you can angle the lower stems downward as well as upward to cover the rim of the basket and build a domed effect on top. This helps to give a unified effect to the floral arrangement and container.

2 Trim the viburnum and hosta leaf stems so they are roughly twice the height of the basket and press them into the foam at an angle (p45).

3 Add the stocks next, as they are quite architectural and will help to create the correct overall shape of the arrangement. Space the stocks evenly throughout the foliage frame.

4 Add the roses next, and lastly the marguerites, as they have the most delicate stems. Keep these stems a little taller than the others to break the domed contour of the arrangement and soften it a little.

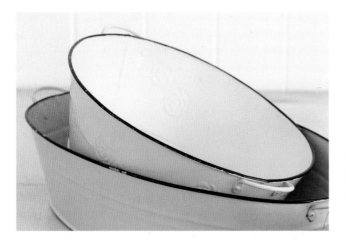

OVAL BASKETS
Look out for different sizes of these useful oval-shaped baskets to suit different locations. They also work well when potted up with bulbs as spring arrangements.

← 5 white Solomon seal

← 3 cream stocks

← 3 white stocks

↓ 2 long garden viburnum stems (cut into smaller-stemmed sprays)

8 marguerites →

6 'Vendela' → cream single roses

↑ 6 'Avalanche' white single roses

↓ 10 alchemilla

7 hosta → leaves

Other materials

Enamel basket (12in/30cm long)
1–2 blocks floral foam (plastic tray and florist's tape optional) or chicken wire
Florist's scissors

Possible substitutions

Veronicas (for stocks); peonies (for single roses); spray roses (for marguerites)

FLORAL CUPCAKES

The aim of this design is to recreate a sugary pink confection that looks almost like a three-tiered wedding cake. It would make a delightful focal point as the table centerpiece for a summer tea party, bridal shower, baby shower, or even a christening, and the color or variety of flowers can, of course, change according to the reason for the celebration. If you don't have a wire cupcake stand such as this, use a tiered glass or ceramic cake stand and weave a couple of trails of ivy around the stem of the handle or the base. Any leftover blooms can be arranged in pretty teacups and used as individual place settings at the table. The blooms should last for five days if you keep the flowers in good condition (pp34–35).

HOW TO ARRANGE

1 To cover the central stem of the stand, cut a block of soaked floral foam into lengths that will fit in between the tiers of the stand. Cut each length in half, place the two halves on either side of the stem, and press them together. If necessary, tape the two pieces together with florist's tape to secure them. Pin pieces of flat moss over the foam to hide it, then wrap the ivy trails around the moss-covered foam (see below).

2 Half-fill each tea light holder with water. Cut the flower stems down so that the flower heads sit just above the rim of each tea light holder. Arrange enough blooms to cover the cake stand (odd numbers look better).

3 Arrange the flowers in their tea light holders on the stand in a random way—don't worry about putting big blooms at the bottom and the smallest at the top, as this all-round arrangement looks better if it is quite organic.

DECORATED STAND
The handle that runs through the center of this tiered cake stand has been covered in floral foam, moss, and ivy to form a textured green backdrop to the individual blooms.

Flowers and foliage

↓ 2 large pink hydrangeas cut into 11 small flower heads

↓ 11 pale pink single roses

↓ 11 blush-pink peonies

↑ flat moss

↑ 4 trailing ivy stems

Other materials

Cake stand
1 tea light holder per flower head (approximately 33 holders)
1 block floral foam
Craft knife
Florist's tape
Pins
Florist's scissors

Possible substitutions

Sweet peas (for any of the flowers). Use three stems per tea light holder

SUMMER BOUQUET

This large, lush bouquet captures the delightful variety and beauty of a fragrant summer garden. Although—as with any hand-tied bouquet—it's important to create a domed effect when arranging these flowers, as this collection will look better if it is gathered in a slightly looser and more random way to recreate the feel of a full flower bed. It makes a wonderful thank-you gift or birthday present, and should last about seven days if you keep the flowers in good condition (pp34–35).

HOW TO ARRANGE

1 Sort the different flowers and foliage into separate piles. Choose a dominant flower, such as a rose or peony, and hold its stem in one hand. Add another variety of flower to it, twisting the bunch around slightly in your hand.

2 Add one of each of the different flowers and foliage at the same angle to create a spiral stem effect and keep turning the bunch around in the same direction as you work. Allow the spiked tip of the lysimachia to extend beyond the curved contour of the arrangement to break it up a little. Check the flowers to make sure they are spread out equally around the arrangement.

3 Continue adding the different stems in turn at the same angle, and arrange the last stems at a lower angle to create a domed effect.

4 Tie the arrangement at the binding point with twine and secure it in a knot.

5 Trim the ends of the stems at an angle so they are roughly the same length and will all be able to sit in water. Leave the bouquet in fresh water until you give it away.

Flowers and foliage

5 spearmint → stems with flowers

↓ 10 alchemilla

8 single → salmon pink roses

← 8–9 lysimachia

5 pale pink → peonies

↓ 5 salal stems

5 senecio stems →

← 10 mixed sweet peas

Other materials

Twine or garden string
Florist's scissors

Possible substitutions

Small-headed hydrangeas (for peonies); veronica (for lysimachia); Eucalyptus (for salal); summer herbs (for senecio)

SUMMER GARDEN BLOOMS
This detail highlights the delicate nature of summer sweet pea and peony petals. Their appealing fragility is accentuated by furry silver-green senecio, spearmint, and lime-green alchemilla.

SUMMER FANTASY

A well-designed herbaceous border can create order and harmony from a disparate range of plant shapes, heights, and colors. It's this creative containment of the diversity and complexity of nature that is the inspiration behind this urban take on a cottage garden. The various levels and stages of a flower bed are recreated with different blooms in thin, oblong troughs containing recycled plastic bottles (p31) and angular glass containers.

EFFECT This design, with its carefully planned, graduated structure and height is an exciting way of bringing a summer garden in full bloom indoors.

COLOR Soft hues of blue, pink, mauve, and purple recreate the pastel shades of a traditional summer border, while a splash of strong pink provides a lively focal point.

SHAPE We've used spear- and globe-shaped flowers *en masse* to create an architectural look to the overall design. Flowers with the shortest stems sit at the front of the display.

COUNTRY SUMMER WEDDING

This mix of blooms and foliage is lightly scented, full of texture, and reminiscent of the countryside in midsummer. Many of these ingredients, such as the herbs, alchemilla, and ivy trails, can be picked straight from the garden. The shape of the bouquet and pew end—a teardrop—is a slightly more romantic style for a country wedding.

BOUTONNIERE

1 pink single rose
1 white leaf stem
1 rosemary sprig

BOUQUET

10 mauve sweet peas
6 pink single roses
4 lilac and purple lisianthus
5 campanula 'Glomerata'
5 alchemilla stems
6 purple veronica
3 trailing ivy stems
6 white leaf stems
7 rosemary sprigs

PEW END

9 purple veronica
5 purple lisianthus
10 alchemilla
7 pink spray roses
10 privet stems

TABLE CENTERPIECE

1 bunch miniature hebe sprigs
1 small bunch sage stems
1 small bunch rosemary sprigs
1 small bunch peppermint stems
9 purple veronica
6 pink spray roses
7 pink single roses

↓ pink single roses

↓ campanula 'Glomerata'

← pink spray roses

↓ rosemary sprigs

↓ trailing ivy stems

← pepper stems

← lilac lisianthus

← miniature hebe sprigs

← purple veronica

← sage stems

← privet stems

↑ purple lisianthus

↑ mauve sweet peas

← alchemilla stems

← white leaf

BOUTONNIERE

This single rose boutonniere is meant to match the color of the roses in the bride's bouquet; keep a pink single rose aside for every boutonniere that you need to make up.

1 Wire the rose, white leaf, and rosemary according to the step-by-steps for wiring a boutonniere in section 1 (pp48–51).

2 Mist the rose occasionally to keep it fresh until it is needed, then supply it with a pin to attach it onto the lapel of a jacket.

BOUQUET

A teardrop bouquet is arranged a little differently to that of a typical hand-tied wedding bouquet, and is deliberately looser and softer.

1 Prop a mirror against a wall at an angle and stand in front of it so you can see the bunch clearly reflected back at you as you work.

2 Divide the different ingredients into separate piles. Start with the longest stems—one of each of the alchemillas, roses, and ivy. Hold them in one hand at the binding point. This is the base of your bunch. Add smaller blooms on top and out to the sides, inserting them into the binding point at an angle to create a spiral effect without turning the bunch at all.

3 Add bigger blooms to this framework, building the curved contour of the bouquet back toward you. Arrange the ivy trails and white leaf sprigs so that they rise a little higher than the other stems.

4 Secure the bunch with a length of raffia and then cover the raffia with a piece of entwined seagrass tied in a pretty knot. Trim the stem ends straight across with shears.

PEW END

This teardrop pew end, which echoes the shape of the bridal bouquet and uses many of the same flowers, is a floral foam arrangement.

1 Make two holes in the top of a shallow tray and loop a piece of wire through them to attach the arrangement onto the end of the pew (p203). Press a soaked square of foam into the tray and tape the two together with florist's tape.

2 If you have a plank of wood, hammer a nail into it and hang the tray temporarily. These pew ends will be viewed from the front and above, so it helps if each tray is at the right angle when you arrange the flowers.

3 Arrange the flowers and foliage according to the step-by-steps for a floral foam arrangement in section 1 (pp44–47). Like the bouquet (previous page), a few stems at the base of the arrangement should be about twice as long as those around the sides and on top. If you make this the day before the wedding, mist the flowers after arranging, and again once you have attached the trays to the pew ends.

TABLE CENTERPIECE

Like the wedding bouquet, this table centerpiece is a romantic display full of scent and texture, but this time arranged in a rustic, earthenware container. If you have any roses left over after arranging the blooms, pull the petals off gently and scatter them randomly around the base of the vase just before the wedding guests arrive.

1 Cut a block of soaked floral foam so it fits inside a 7in (19cm) high glazed earthenware container. It should also sit 2in (5cm) above the lip so the foliage stems can be inserted at an upward angle to hide the rim of the container. Press the foliage in at angles to form a framework. Arrange sprigs of hebe in clumps.

2 Add the big pink single roses next and space them evenly throughout the arrangement.

3 Cut small-stemmed pink spray roses from the main stems and place them next.

4 Add the spears of veronica last of all. Fill any gaps with extra sprigs of sage or rosemary.

SWEET PEAS

This small vase arrangement illustrates the "less is more" principle perfectly (pp12–13). A few mixed sweet peas loosely arranged in a covered glass tumbler may not initially seem special, but the intimate scale of this design and the subtle hues of the delicate petals soon begin to radiate and provide a wonderful sensory delight. And, although they have small, fragile flowers, sweet peas have a light, fragrant perfume that is irresistible. This display looks exquisite in a bedroom or on a dressing table, and will last for two or three days.

HOW TO ARRANGE

1 Place a length of raffia on a flat surface and lay a hosta leaf over it so that the raffia runs beneath the middle of the leaf.

2 Lay a tall glass tumbler or small straight-sided vase on its side on top of a hosta leaf. Cover the surface of the vase with the other hosta leaves so that they slightly overlap each other. Wrap the two ends of raffia around the leaves and tie them in a knot. You may need to add a second raffia tie if the vase is tall. Trim the bottom of the leaves and stalk ends so that they align with the base of the vase. These leaves give the vase a slightly quirky look that makes an interesting contrast with the endless curves of the sweet peas.

3 Fill two-thirds of the vase with water and arrange the sweet pea stems in an informal style to give an all-around display. The blooms won't last long, so if you grow sweet peas in your garden replace them with fresh stems every few days.

Flowers and foliage

← 2 pink sweet peas

↓ 2 purple sweet peas

2 dark pink → sweet peas

2 light purple → sweet peas

2 lilac sweet peas →

← 3 hosta leaves

SIMPLE ALTERNATIVE
If you have no time to cover a vase, arrange the stems in several old-fashioned wine glasses and place them in a row on a table or along a shelf.

Other materials

Tall glass tumbler (6½in/16.5cm) or small straight-sided vase
Raffia
Florist's scissors

Possible substitutions

Peonies or spray roses

HYDRANGEA BALL

Minimal ingredients create maximum impact with this simple vase arrangement. The aim is to work with a limited palette of colors and flowers, and not to fill the bowl up to the rim with petals. Hydrangeas are ideal for this design, as they are one of the few flowers whose petals are coarse enough to tolerate sitting in water; most are too thin and delicate, and soon turn slimy. It's worth trying to find something similar to this twisted, woven ring of dried vine around the base of the bowl, as it brings added interest and another natural element to the display. This design looks good on a coffee table or in a modern bathroom and will last for a week if you refresh the water and recut the stems.

HOW TO ARRANGE

1 Pour a small amount of water into the fishbowl—the water should only be about 2in (5cm) deep.

2 Cut the stems of three of the flower heads slightly shorter and arrange them first, placing the ends of the stems in the water.

3 Take the remaining three flower heads and carefully insert their slightly longer stems in between the bottom layer of flowers until the stems sit in the water. The lower layer of flower heads should help to keep these uppermost blooms stable in this all-around display. Fluff out the hydrangea petals so they are not squashed.

Flowers

↓ 6 pink hydrangea flower heads

A NATURAL BASE
A ring of twisted vine adds texture and interest to this flower arrangement.

Other materials

Fishbowl (16in/41cm high)
Florist's scissors
Woven vine base or similar

Possible substitution

Gypsophila

DELICATE DRAMA
Hydrangeas, with their impressive size, dense shape, and multiple petals, are a perfect example of "less is more." Misting is an excellent way of keeping the petals fresh, as they absorb the water.

DELPHINIUMS AND HYDRANGEAS IN BLUE

A striking, architectural, front-facing vase arrangement such as this needs air and space around it to give the right impression, and the visual impact is greater if the vase is the same color as the flowers. The hydrangea stems are much shorter than those of the grasses and delphiniums, so ensure that the level of water is always topped up. This front-facing arrangement is best situated on a hall table or in a light, minimalist conservatory or living room, and should last at least a week if you keep the flowers in good condition (pp34–35).

HOW TO ARRANGE

1 Fill two-thirds of the vase with water. Trim the delphinium stems so they are all the same length and arrange them so that they flare out naturally to the sides and their mixed colors are evenly distributed.

2 Tuck the hydrangea stems just inside the front rim of the vase and wedge them in slightly so that they stay in place.

3 Rearrange the delphiniums if necessary until you are happy with their overall shape and balance. Trim the grass stems so that they are a little shorter than the delphiniums and insert them in between the delphiniums and hydrangeas to link the different blooms together.

VISUAL CONTRASTS
Fluttery sprays of tall green grasses with trailing leaves help to break up the intense blue of the flowers.

Flowers and foliage

← 15 'Panicum' fountain grasses

10 'Blue Bee' delphiniums ↓

← 10 'Double Blue' delphiniums

← 10 blue hydrangeas

Other materials

Blue flared glass vase (16in/41cm high)
Florist's scissors

Possible substitutions

Larkspur or aconitum (for delphinium), large-headed chrysanthemums (for hydrangea), spear grass (for fountain grass)

FOLIAGE AND SEED HEAD DISPLAY

It's not often that you see vase arrangements constructed almost entirely from foliage, but with the right shapes and textures they look fabulous. This display expresses the lushness of midsummer, and would look stunning in an airy, white sunroom, a contemporary space, or in a hall positioned on a white or clear plinth or tall table. There are several different ingredients in this arrangement, so it won't make much difference to the overall design if you can't find one or two of them. It should last for ten days (pp34–35).

HOW TO ARRANGE

1 Trim the stalks from the two monstera leaves and use them to line the sides of the vase. Scrunch up a large square or two of cellophane and press it down toward the base of the vase. The cellophane helps to hold the leaves in place and give extra height to the foliage; if the foliage stems are long, pack the cellophane down hard.

Foliage

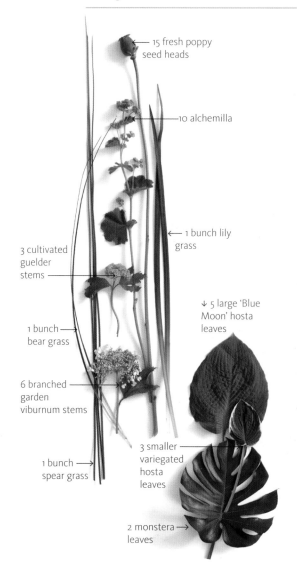

15 fresh poppy seed heads

10 alchemilla

1 bunch lily grass

3 cultivated guelder stems

↓ 5 large 'Blue Moon' hosta leaves

1 bunch bear grass

6 branched garden viburnum stems

3 smaller variegated hosta leaves

1 bunch spear grass

2 monstera leaves

Other materials

Tall clear column vase (16in/41cm high)
Florist's scissors
Cellophane
Elastic bands

Possible substitutions

For a darker colored display use: red robin (for viburnum); copper beech (for guelder rose); leucadendron (for poppy seed heads); hypericum (for alchemilla); black tie leaves (for hosta leaves)

2 Fill two-thirds of the vase with water. Divide the different grasses into bunches of 5 to 6 blades, tie them with small elastic bands, and trim the ends.

3 Arrange the first three hosta leaves evenly in the vase to provide the base for the foliage.

4 Add the garden viburnum to build up an all-round framework of stems. Then add the cultivated guelder.

5 Add the poppy heads, spacing them evenly through the arrangement. They should sit a little higher than the viburnum heads so they rise above the other foliage.

6 Arrange the lily and bear grass bundles at angles around the sides of the arrangement so they fall at a natural angle. Add bunches of spear grass through the center to create extra height.

7 Add the alchemilla next, using them to fill any gaps and seamlessly link the various colors and textures together.

8 Place the variegated hosta leaves at either side of the arrangement as a final touch; move the foliage heads slightly to make suitable spaces for them. Top the water up to the rim of the vase.

URBAN CHIC SUMMER WEDDING

Although peonies may have a lingering reputation for being quite traditional, their handsome, well-defined shape and the intense, glossy color of their petals make them perfect for a modern early-summer wedding. Their great advantage is that they won't disintegrate and fall apart easily if the wedding day is hot or windy.

BOUTONNIERE

1 'Aqua' single rose
1 stem senecio with closed buds

BOUQUET

9 dark pink double-headed peonies

PEW END

8 dark pink double-headed peonies

TABLE CENTERPIECE

4 hosta leaves
4 dark pink peonies
4 pale pink 'Sarah Bernhardt'
   peonies
5 'Aqua' single roses

← 'Aqua' single rose

↓ dark pink peonies

pale pink → 'Sarah Bernhardt' peonies

↓ senecio stems with closed buds

↓ hosta leaves

BOUTONNIERE

Choose a rose close in color to the bouquet (a peony would be too big as a boutonniere). Small curls of black ribbon are tucked in between the rose and senecio leaves for interest.

1 Wire the rose and senecio according to the step-by-steps for wiring a boutonniere in section 1 (pp48–51). Remove any outer petals from the rose if it looks too large for a boutonniere.

2 Cut three 1½in (4cm) lengths of black ribbon. Fold each length in half, pinch the ends together and wire them with a double leg mount (p48). Trim the wires and cover them with stem tape.

3 Group the ribbon curls at the side of the rose, arrange the senecio leaves behind them, trim the wires, and bind them altogether with stem tape. Press the tape down with your fingers to secure it. Supply it with a pin to attach it to the lapel of a jacket

BOUQUET

The impact of this stylish bridal bouquet is all the greater because of its minimalism; these blowsy peonies need nothing else to show them off to perfection.

1 Hold the stem of one flower in your hand and add another stem to it, twisting the stems around slightly in one direction in your hand as you do so.

2 Add more stems at the same angle to create a spiral stem effect. Keep turning the bunch around in the same direction as you work.

3 Arrange the last layer of flowers a little lower around the edges for a slightly domed effect. Don't worry if there are slight gaps between the flowers—it's quite hard to gather these large blooms tightly together.

4 Holding the bunch in one hand, secure it with a length of raffia. Then cover the raffia binding with a length of black ribbon tied in a bow.

5 Cut the stem ends straight across with garden shears so they are all the same, short length and won't get entangled in the bride's dress.

PEW END

Frothy peonies in pale pink paper cones look almost like giant ice cream cones, and add a sense of irresistible delight to what is a minimal, stylish display.

1 For each cone, curl a piece of thick cardstock into a trumpet shape and staple it at the back. (Use black if you want to match the ribbons and vase, or very thick textured paper for white cones.)

2 Cut two short slits in the back of each cone, weave two lengths of raffia in and out of these slits, and attach them to the pew ends.

3 Pack cellophane inside the base of the cone to prevent the flowers slipping too low, and to help create the right shape.

4 Attach a vial of water to each of eight peonies in full flower. Arrange the slightly taller stems at the back of the cone and shorter stems at the front to form a graduated, curved effect that repeats the shape of the bride's bouquet.

TABLE CENTERPIECE

Peonies and roses need the sharp, clean lines of a black cube vase to give them a modern, uncluttered feel.

1 Fill a vase (5½in/14cm diameter and height) with water and mold chicken wire inside the vase (p37). Insert a hosta leaf through the chicken wire at each corner of the vase.

2 Insert four of the roses at an angle through the wire so that each rose rests on a hosta leaf. Place a dark pink peony in between each rose, then add four pale pink peonies to create a second layer. Rest the final rose at the top to give the arrangement a slightly stylized pyramid shape.

MAXIMUM IMPACT
A mass of different colors in an arrangement can sometimes be confusing and distracting. Keeping to a limited palette of colors and flower varieties gives this arrangement dynamic impact.

SUNFLOWER VASE

The loosely arranged sunflowers in this rustic, burlap-covered column vase are massed to give a sense of organic growth—almost as if they are still growing in a field—and together they create a strong, textural look. This modern design is all about using your own visual judgement to create a basic domed shape with added height and shorter flowers that hide any unsightly stems from view. It should last for ten days (pp34–35).

HOW TO ARRANGE

1 Place the burlap fabric on a table and lay the vase on its side on the fabric. Fold the fabric around the vase, then secure a double length of seagrass around the vase and tie it in a knot. Stand the vase upright, rearrange the burlap folds, and bind them against the sides of the vase with as many diagonal double lengths of seagrass as you think you need.

2 Half-fill the vase with water. Strip all the leaves from the sunflower stems so the flower heads don't droop.

3 Hold a sunflower in one hand and add a few blooms to it, twisting the stems around slightly in one direction in your hand as you do so to create a rough spiral effect. Add a few more stems, then trim them to approximately the same length. Instead of tying the stems together at this point, drop them straight into the vase. This loose spiral arrangement provides a criss-cross framework to support the remaining stems.

4 Add some taller stems at the back and shorter stems at the front and sides to hide the neck of the vase and any visible stems. Aim to achieve an organic, not tight, look. Nip off any extra leaves beneath the flower heads. Then top up the vase almost to the rim with water.

Flowers

← 11 giant sunflowers

↓ 9 'Teddy Bear' sunflowers

← 9 black sunflowers

Other materials

Column vase (16in/41cm high)
Burlap fabric or sacking material
 (approx 4ft x 20in/1.2m x 50cm)
Seagrass cord
Florist's scissors

Possible substitutions

Large-headed chrysanthemums
 (for all sunflower varieties)

RICH TEXTURE
This mass of sunflower varieties butting up to each other creates
a gloriously rich textural tapestry: their variation in shape and the
configuration of their petals make for a compelling display.

AUTUMN BOUQUET

This spiral hand-tied bouquet captures many of the rich colors and textures of autumn flowers and foliage. Celosia flower heads are heavy and easier to use in a compact bouquet where they are supported by other blooms, so use quite a high binding point to arrange these flowers and foliage. If you can't find cotinus, the bouquet will still look striking with any variety of green foliage. Give it away as a gift, or put it in a rustic container and place it at the center of a table set for Sunday lunch. It will last for at least seven days if you keep the flowers in good condition (pp34–35).

HOW TO ARRANGE

1 Sort the flowers and foliage into individual piles. Hold the stem of one flower, such as a celosia, in your hand at the binding point and arrange three to four stems of salal around it. Add another variety of flower at an angle, twisting the stems around slightly in one direction in your hand.

2 Add one of each of all the flowers and foliage at the same angle to create a spiral stem effect, turning the arrangement in the same direction as you do so. Look at the top of the bouquet to check that you like the arrangement of blooms, then add the remaining stems. Cut the stems down a little if they are becoming hard to handle. Arrange the last two layers of flowers and foliage a little lower around the edges to create a slightly domed effect. Add a few stems of salal around the edges of the bouquet to frame the flowers.

3 Tie the arrangement with raffia or garden string secured in a knot.

4 Cut the stems straight across with a pair of garden shears so that they are all the same length. If the bouquet is a gift, keep the stems in water until you give it away.

INSIDER TIP

• **Cotinus is long-stemmed**; the lower half has bigger leaves while the upper part bears small leaves, and both create good texture. It's a shame to waste the lower part, so cut the stems in half and use both parts in arrangements.

Flowers and foliage

7 alstroemeria ↓

↓ 7 orange spray roses

↓ 5 protea

↓ 6 hypericum berry stems

6 cotinus stems↓

↑ 5 red celosia

← 6 salal stems

Other materials

Florist's scissors
Raffia or garden string
Garden shears

Possible substitutions

Trachelium (for celosia); roses (for protea); freesias (for spray roses); eryngium (for alstroemeria)

SCULPTURAL FLOWERS
Exotic flowers are often very bright and striking in appearance, and tend to last well. Exotic varieties, such as these protea, create a strong, sculptural effect when paired with other blooms.

FRUIT CUBE

The unusual decorative effect of the container in this bold, graphic vase arrangement has been achieved by placing one cube vase inside another and filling the gaps with slices of lime. The secret is to use two vases that are only slightly different in size and that fit together neatly. Arrange this display on the day that you need it, as the juice from the limes tends to seep out after a while. The compact nature of celosia flowers means that it is easiest to make them up as a hand-tied bouquet before you place them in the vase. This little arrangement should last for two or three days, and will work well on a shelf in a small enclosed room or a kitchen or bathroom, as the limes create a lovely light scent.

HOW TO ARRANGE

1 Place one cube vase inside the other, slice the limes with a sharp knife, and slot them into the gap between the vases. Use the knife to edge them into place on all four sides. Fill the inner vase only with water.

2 Trim all the foliage from the celosia stems so the large flower heads with their undulating, rippling surface area provide all the focus and texture. Arrange the stems in a simple spiral bouquet with a high binding point to give a compact look. Alternate each color as you build up the domed shape of the bouquet, and turn the bouquet in the same direction as you work. Manipulate the flower heads slightly by pressing them together to eliminate any gaps.

3 When you have added all the celosia, trim the stems so they can all sit in water, tie the bunch securely with raffia or garden string, and place it in the inner vase.

Flowers and fruit

8 red celosia →

← 4 fresh limes

← 8 green celosia

CITRUS SPACE
Build up horizontal rows of lime slices to fill the gap in between the two vases.

Other materials

1 large glass cube vase
 (6 x 6in/15 x 15cm)
1 slightly smaller glass cube vase
 (4½ x 4½in/11.5 x 11.5cm)
Sharp knife
Florist's scissors
Raffia or garden string

Possible substitutions

Sunflowers (for celosia); lemons
 (for limes)

COMPACT CLUSTER
These orange and green celosia, with their dense, ruffled flower heads, provide texture and depth when grouped *en masse*. They are large-headed flowers, so only a few are needed for an impact.

ORANGE FISHBOWL

The iridescent color of the fishbowl in this contemporary all-round vase arrangement sets the tone for the eclectic mix of autumnal flowers and foliage that rest on top of it. It is designed to be compact yet quite loose and unstructured to create a contrast with the very smooth, uniform curves of the bowl; chicken wire placed inside the bowl helps to keep the stems at the right angle. This design will provide a bright injection of color in a modern kitchen, bathroom, sunroom, or office boardroom and should last for at least a week if you keep the flowers in good condition (pp34–35).

HOW TO ARRANGE

1 Place the chicken wire inside the bowl and half-fill the bowl with water.

2 Cut down the long stems of cotinus and use a few of the shorter stems to create a basic framework.

3 Add a few dahlias around the edge of the bowl, then add a second layer of dahlias so they appear to almost rest on the lower layer. Add a few more stems of cotinus to break up the blooms if they look too dense.

4 Add the gloriosa lilies, placing them evenly around the arrangement. Their elongated petals add an elegant contrast to the round puff-ball effect of the dahlias, so the lilies should sit slightly higher than the other blooms. Then fill the bowl to the top with more water.

Flowers and foliage

← 5 stems cotinus

← 5 orange dahlias

7 gloriosa lilies ↑ with short stems

← 5 yellow dahlias

Other materials

Orange fishbowl (8in/20cm high)
Chicken wire
Florist's scissors

Possible substitutions

Sunflowers and celosia (for dahlias); upright amaranthus (for gloriosa lilies); lilies (for cotinus)

JEWEL DAHLIAS

This mass of dahlias is designed to create a sensational impact: their intricate petal formations and intense colors shine like jewels in an old jewelry box, while the mix of buds, semi-open, and fully open blooms add interest and texture. Whether you gather dahlias from the garden or buy them, ensure their strong colors mix harmoniously together and don't clash. This display will look lovely on a chest of drawers, a traditional writing desk, or a hall table, and should last for a week or more (pp34–35).

HOW TO ARRANGE

1 Line the inside of the box with cellophane or a similar material. Cut the tops off four water bottles (or more or less, depending on how large your box is) and arrange them so they fill the box. Arrange chicken wire in the two rear bottles for the taller flowers, then half-fill all the bottles with water.

2 Arrange some stems at the back first: trim the stems so the flower heads cluster together just below the edge of the box lid, and arrange them in the bottles so they rest against the opened lid. Use the chicken wire to guide their angle and position. Place about five stems in each bottle.

3 Cut the stems slightly shorter as you fill up the front of the bottles at the back, and shorter still for the bottles at the front, to create a graduated effect. Arrange some shorter-stemmed flowers at the sides, too, to create an even effect. Put the wooden box in position and top up the bottles with water.

SIMPLE EQUIPMENT
Use cellophane to catch any drips and protect the lining of the box, and chicken wire inside the bottles to provide effective support for the flowers.

Flowers

↓ 5 'Black Fox' dahlias

↓ 5 'Boy Scout' dahlias

5 'Red Fox' dahlias ↓

↓ 5 'Stratus' dahlias

5 'Red Cap' dahlias →

Other materials

Old wooden box or similar
  (approx 12 x 8in/30 x 20cm)
Cellophane
4 large plastic water bottles
Chicken wire
Florist's scissors

Possible substitutions

Large and small sunflowers,
  big-bloomed chrysanthemums,
  hydrangeas

HARMONIOUS HUES
Although these are all strong colors, they sit next to each other on a color wheel, so they harmonize well and have a pleasing effect when mixed together in an arrangement.

VEGETABLE AND FRUIT BOUQUET

As summer turns to fall and harvest time, an improvised hand-tied bouquet of ingredients from the garden or even a local market makes a wonderfully evocative centerpiece for a dining table or kitchen table. Any fruit or vegetable with a very short stalk can be wired, and those with no stalk at all can be supported on a garden stake. This bouquet is slightly smaller because these ingredients are heavier to hold and support than the usual flowers and foliage. It should last for three to four days in water with regular misting.

HOW TO ARRANGE

1 To wire a broccoli floret, insert one end of a thick piece of 90 gauge wire through the side of the stalk, bend the end down and twist it around the rest of the wire in a double leg mount (pp48–51). The length of wire should align with the stalk. To prepare the limes, push a garden stake into the base of each fruit.

2 Sort the ingredients into separate piles (reserve the cabbage leaves until the end). Hold a broccoli floret in one hand at the binding point, which should be quite high up so that the bunch remains compact. Place one of each of the other ingredients around the floret, turning the bunch in the same direction as you work. Arrange the rosemary so that it rises a little higher above the rest of the ingredients and upturn the spring onions to show their white bulbs and roots.

3 Add another of each ingredient to the bouquet, turning it in the same direction each time. If the bouquet begins to feel heavy, tie it together at the binding point so that it is more manageable to hold. Add the rest of the ingredients.

4 Arrange the cabbage leaves around the outside of the bunch to frame it. Tie the bouquet at the binding point, fill an earthenware pot or a similar rustic container with water, and place the bouquet in the pot.

Flowers, fruit, and vegetables

6 wired → broccoli florets

↓ 9 spring onions tied in bunches of three

↓ 5 lilac dahlias

↓ 5 sage stems

↓ 3 trachelium

↙ 5 sprays unripe blackberries

↓ 5 sedum

↑ 8 rosemary sprigs

↑ 3 limes on garden stakes

3 cabbage → leaves

Other materials

Earthenware pot or similar
90 gauge wire
Garden stakes
Garden string
Florist's scissors

Possible substitutions

Cauliflower (for broccoli);
 elderberries (for blackberries);
 asparagus (for spring onions);
 any fresh herbs

AUTUMN WEDDING

Rich autumnal blooms of amber, gold, russet, and red predominate in these autumn wedding arrangements. They are bright and striking, but arranged in quite an informal way to give a rustic look. Sprays of blackberries bring a country feel to each design, but ensure that you use unripe berries (ripe berries drop off easily, and can stain clothing).

BOUTONNIERE

1 'Pinky Flair' hypericum
1 unripe blackberry spray
3 ivy leaves
1 orange calla lily

BOUQUET

7 calla lilies
9 unripe blackberry sprays
11 'Pinky Flair' hypericum
6 'Cherry Brandy' single roses
8 'Sonia' sunflowers

PEW END

6 'Excellent Flair' hypericum
6 'Pinky Flair' hypericum
7 unripe blackberry sprays
12 'Sonia' sunflowers

TABLE CENTERPIECE

4 'Excellent Flair' hypericum
4 'Pinky Flair' hypericum
7 unripe blackberry sprays
8 'Sonia' sunflowers
6 'Cherry Brandy' single roses
5 cotinus stems
5 ivy stems

↓ cotinus

← 'Pinky Flair' hypericum

↓ 'Cherry Brandy' single roses

↓ 'Excellent Flair' hypericum

↓ orange calla lilies

↓ unripe blackberry sprays

↓ ivy stems

↑ 'Sonia' sunflowers

BOUTONNIERE

The unusual mango color and swirled shape of this calla lily makes it an interesting variation on a classic rose boutonniere. The sprays of blackberries and hypericum berries add a delightful detail.

1 Wire the calla lily, hypericum berries, unripe blackberries, and ivy leaves according to the step-by-steps in section 1 (pp48–51).

2 Group the wired foliage around the wired lily stem in a graduated sequence, trim the wires, wrap stem tape around all the wires, and press the tape down with your fingers to seal it.

3 Mist the calla lily occasionally to keep it fresh until it is needed, then supply it with a pin to attach it onto the lapel of a jacket.

BOUQUET

This bouquet uses miniature sunflowers; larger sunflowers would overpower the arrangement. This means that it retains a delicate, pretty feel, even though its colours are quite strong.

1 Divide the different ingredients into separate piles. Begin with a rose or calla lily and place one of each of the ingredients around it at an angle to create a spiral stem effect with a high binding point to give a compact look. Turn the bunch in the same direction as you add each stem.

2 Add one of each of the different flowers until you have included all the blooms and they are balanced equally throughout the bouquet. Arrange the last two layers of flowers slightly lower around the edges for a domed effect.

3 Secure the bunch with string or raffia, then take a very long piece of raffia, fold it four times to create eight strands and make them into a bow. Attach the bow to the bouquet with a small piece of raffia. Trim the ends of the stems straight across with a pair of secateurs.

PEW END

The arrangement is designed to be a simpler version of the wedding bouquet: it contains fewer flowers, but includes another variety of hypericum berry. It is arranged in the same way as a spiral bouquet.

1 Divide the different ingredients into separate piles. Hold a sunflower in the middle of the stem (to give a looser look) and place one of each of the ingredients around it at an angle to create a spiral stem effect. Rather than turning the bunch, make it up facing you. Place the flowers at the back slightly higher up to give a graduated, not domed, effect.

2 When you have added one of each of all the different ingredients, repeat the sequence until you have included all the flowers and foliage and they are balanced equally throughout the arrangement.

3 Tie the arrangement with a length of string or raffia and secure it in a knot. Then take a very long piece of raffia, fold it four times to create eight strands and make them into a bow. Attach the bow to the bouquet with a small piece of raffia. Trim the stem ends straight across with a pair of garden shears so they are all the same length.

TABLE CENTERPIECE

This informal basket centerpiece has a watertight container tucked snugly inside it that acts like a vase, while chicken wire inside the rim of the container ensures that all the stems are angled in the right direction. It's important to keep all the stems short in this arrangement so that the proportions of the flowers and foliage match the size and shape of the basket.

1 Place a watertight container inside a 12in (30cm) round wicker basket. Arrange the chicken wire inside the container and fill the container with water. Create a skeleton framework of foliage with short stems of ivy. These stems should be angled so that their leaves fall softly over the sides of the bowl.

2 Add short stems of cotinus to give even coverage through the framework without it being overfull.

3 Add the roses next, as they are the biggest flower heads. Arrange them evenly through the arrangement.

4 Add the blackberries and hypericum and then the sunflowers to finish.

FALL FANTASY

Inspired by 18th-century Dutch works of art, this sumptuous display of autumn blooms and harvest fruits looks almost like a still life painting itself. The abundance of lilies, roses, crocosmia, rudbeckia, cotinus, bull rushes, and wired fruits is given a dramatic flourish by a large traditional pedestal urn, a swathe of deep maroon silk draped around the urn, and an intense shot of color from the amaranthus that trails onto the table beside the scattered fruits.

COLOR A palette of typical autumn colors is used to represent this changing season as the leaves outdoors turn from green to fiery oranges, reds, and crimsons.

EFFECT The inclusion of fruit and fabric as well as flowers and foliage turns this design into one of rich delights, even extravagance, although all these individual elements are, in fact, very ordinary.

SHAPE The flared pedestal urn allows the flowers to form a handsome fan shape. Softer flower shapes are used at the edges, while a cluster of fruits in the center draws the eye right in.

FOLIAGE AND BERRY WREATH

This lovely, natural-looking autumnal wired wreath of complementary and harmonious colors actually includes some dyed leaves to give the best effect: the dye almost preserves the fresh leaves so they don't turn dry and brittle (although if they get wet they can stain paintwork). The base of the wreath is built up with moss, which is a better option than floral foam, as it is lighter and has more depth at the side to attach the foliage. As with all arrangements, turn the wire frame around as you pack in the moss so that the section you work on is always in front of you. Either hang the wreath, unadorned, on a wall or propped up on a mantelpiece, or attach a bow and hang it on a door. You can also lay it flat in the middle of a table and place a candle in the center. It should last for two weeks.

Flowers and foliage

← 12 dyed beech stems

← 4 dyed eucalyptus stems

↓ 12 miniature hebe stems

12 dyed oak leaf stems →

↑ 8 pepper berry sprays

1 large bag sphagnum moss →

8 unripe blackberry sprays →

↑ 12 rosemary sprigs

Other materials

Wire wreath frame (12in/30cm in diameter) from a florist
Florist's scissors
1 ball of garden string
22 gauge wire
Ribbon (optional)

Possible substitutions

Berried ivy, natural eucalyptus, silvery eucalyptus pods, wired apples, hypericum, pine, salal (for any of the flowers and foliage)

HOW TO ARRANGE

1 Prepare the foliage: cut the stems down to 5–6in (12–15cm) or so and strip the leaves off the lower 1in (2.5cm) of each stem.

4 Trim the moss with scissors. Cut the string, leaving a length of about 16in (40cm) still attached to the wreath. Make a loop in the string 4in (10cm) from the attached end. Hold the loop in one hand and the tail end in the other and cross them over under the wreath. Bring them back up above the wreath and tie them in a knot. Trim the loose ends.

2 Position the wire frame so the larger ring lies below the smaller ring. Tie the ball of string onto the wire frame at any point and secure it in a knot.

3 Take a large handful of moss, tease it apart slightly, and pack it in between the two rings in a rounded shape. Gather up loose ends as you press the moss into place, then wind the string diagonally around it to keep it in place. Repeat until the frame is covered.

5 If you want to hang the finished wreath, feel for the edge of the frame with your fingers and insert a length of thick wire into the moss, under the frame at an angle, and out the other side. Bring the ends together to make a loop, twist one length of wire around the other, trim the ends, and hide the twisted ends inside the moss. Holding the loop, twist the wreath around twice in the same direction to tighten the base of the loop.

6 Tie the ball of string back onto the wreath at any point. Place three to four beech leaf stems on top of the moss and wrap string tightly over the stems to secure them to the wreath.

7 Turn the wreath around slightly and place a stem of hebe partly over the oak leaves to create a staggered effect. Secure it in place with the string.

8 Add each of the ingredients in turn, placing small bunches of foliage on the sides and top of the moss. Stagger each group of foliage and turn the wreath as you work.

9 When you have added enough foliage to give a well-balanced look, tie off the string in the same way as before: make a double loop, tuck one loop under the wreath, and tie the two single loops together securely.

10 If you spot any gaps in the wreath, or it looks slightly unbalanced in parts, tuck a few pieces of woody-stemmed foliage such as rosemary and hebe in under the string to even it out. Tie the ribbon in a bow and attach it to the frame, if using.

MIXED WINTER ARRANGEMENT

This crisp white and green vase arrangement, with its heavy winter berries, is warmed up gently by exotic cymbidium orchids (these orchids flower on a very long stem, so the individual heads can be cut off and inserted into orchid vials to give them enough height to suit the design). Such a lovely all-around display would look stunning in a hallway, master bedroom, on a dining room table, or on a low coffee table. The soft-stemmed anemones may need replacing after a few days, but the other blooms should last up to 10 days if you keep them in good condition (pp34–35).

HOW TO ARRANGE

1 Place the chicken wire inside the vase and fill the vase with water.

2 Arrange the skimmia stems first. Keep turning the vase around as you add the foliage to create a fully three-dimensional domed effect. Try not to add too much foliage at this stage.

3 Add the single roses next, placing the shorter stems around the edge of the arrangement and longer ones near the center to reinforce the domed effect. The flowers should look ordered and not muddled. Keep turning the vase so it faces you as you add the roses.

4 Arrange the hypericum and spray roses next, spacing them evenly throughout the arrangement. Recess the flowers slightly so that the tips of the skimmia leaves break the curved contours of the blooms. Then add the anemones.

5 Finally, add the cymbidium orchids—they are quite dominant in this design, so it's worth arranging them last to work out where they sit best.

Flowers and foliage

← 6 white spray roses

↓ 5 cymbidium orchids

↓ 10 hypericum berry stems

6 single → white roses

6 white anemones ↓

← 10 skimmia stems

Other materials

Opaque green glazed flared vase (7in/19cm high)
Chicken wire
Florist's scissors

Possible substitutions

Trachelium (for anemonies), mini amaryllis (for spray roses), Singapore orchids (for cymbidium orchids), berried ivy and rosemary (for skimmia)

FESTIVE FLOWERS
These white anemones, with their frosty petals and cool purple centers, are perfect as a focal point against the lime-green berries, orchids, and green foliage of this festive winter display.

ANEMONE TREE

With their richly colored papery petals, anemones almost look as though they are made out of tissue paper, which helps to give a light, delicate edge to this strong design. This spiral bouquet in floral foam would make a lovely centerpiece on a circular hall or dining room table, or on a mantelpiece or chest of drawers. The anemones will last for five days if you keep the foam moist.

HOW TO ARRANGE

1 Sort the different-colored anemones into separate piles. Hold an anemone in one hand at the binding point and add one of each color to it, turning the bunch around slightly in the same direction as you work. Arrange the last flowers at a lower angle around the edges to create a domed effect.

2 Use a length of ribbon that complements the colors of the flowers to tie the arrangement securely. Cut the stems the same length to give an even base.

3 Pack a piece of cellophane or a similar material into the base of the vase to give the anemone stems added height. Place the arrangement in the center of the vase and insert squares of soaked floral foam around the edges of the vase to wedge the stems in place and keep them upright. The top of the foam should sit 1in (2.5cm) below the rim of the vase. Top the vase up with water and hide the foam with a layer of moss.

INSIDER TIPS

• **If moss is difficult to source**, cover the pieces of floral foam with mixed, colored gravel, or shiny black pebbles.

• **The anemones will open up** and grow a little over time. Although this may make the arrangement a little uneven, it will also add interest and movement to the design.

Flowers and foliage

← 50 mixed anemones

← moss

Other materials

Opaque flared vase (6in/15cm high)
Ribbon
Florist's scissors
Cellophane
1 block floral foam
Craft knife

Possible substitution

Mixed spray roses

EUPHORBIA FOUNTAIN

A bounteous display of small fruits line this vase arrangement of vivid orange euphorbia to create an unusual and interesting balance of form and color. The design includes the useful trick of arranging the euphorbia in a cut-down plastic water bottle with chicken wire inside to create the effect of a jet spray of orange petals showering up into the air. The arrangement will look very impressive on a buffet table at a Halloween or Thanksgiving gathering, on a hall table, or in a contemporary white space. It should last for about five days before the fruits begin to look tired; you could then cut the euphorbia stems down and arrange them in a smaller vase for another five days or so.

Flowers and foliage

↓ 20 'Fulgens' orange euphorbia

← 2 punnets crab apples

← 2 containers kumquats

HOW TO ARRANGE

1 Cut the top off the water bottle so that it becomes a straight-sided container, and place the chicken wire inside it. Half-fill the bottle with water and place it inside the center of the vase.

Other materials

Clear glass column vase (12in/30cm high)
1 large plastic water bottle
Chicken wire
Florist's scissors
Garden stake

Possible substitutions

Molucella or cymbidium orchids (for euphorbia), cherries and chestnuts (for crab apples and kumquats)

2 Tip some kumquats into the space between the bottle and the inside of the vase to form a thick layer—two to three rows high—that looks roughly even, but is still quite random. Use a garden stake to adjust the kumquats slightly so that they lie on their sides and conceal the bottle behind.

INSIDER TIPS

• **Euphorbia releases a milky white sap** if its leaves or stem are cut, which can be an irritant to people with sensitive skin. If you have sensitive skin, wear gloves when you handle these flowers.

• **We have chosen to leave the leaves** on the euphorbia stems to add to the "fountain" look. However, they sometimes wither and drop before the flowers fade, so remove the leaves before arranging the euphorbia, if you prefer.

3 Add some crab apples next, distributing them evenly so that they form a layer roughly the same depth as the kumquats. Pick out any crab apples that are damaged, bruised, or shriveled and discard them.

5 Strip off the leaves from the base of each euphorbia stem to the point where the flowers start growing. These stems can be quite short, as the design looks better if you can see the flowers rising out from the rim of the vase. Put four stems into the bottle and let them flare out naturally to the sides and the front and back to build up the basic framework for an all-around arrangement.

4 Add another layer of kumquats, using the garden stake to adjust slightly if necessary, then pour in a final layer of crab apples to fill the vase up to the rim.

6 Arrange the rest of the stems evenly throughout the arrangement and in the center to create height. Keep turning the vase around as you work to achieve an even, graduated shape on all sides. Then top up the bottle with water.

WINTER BOUQUET

We tend to assume that winter is bereft of plants with color and variety, but this beautiful mixed hand-tied bouquet uses species such as berried ivy as a feature rather than as a backdrop to give structure, definition, and interest (the spiral technique is the best way to control the overall shape of these very different blooms). This bouquet is ideal as a gift or as a table centerpiece in a clear glass vase at a dinner party. It will last up to ten days in water if you refresh the water and re-cut the stems.

HOW TO ARRANGE

1 Sort the different ingredients into separate piles. Hold one amaryllis stem gently upright in one hand and encircle it with two or three stems of berried ivy.

2 Add a rose and twist the bunched blooms around slightly in your hand, then add a stem of hypericum. Keep the stems spiraled by adding them all at the same angle and turning the arrangement in the same direction as you work.

3 When you have added one of each of all the different ingredients, check that you are happy with the arrangement of stems by tilting it toward you, or checking it in a mirror. Trim the stems if necessary if the bouquet is becoming unwieldy in your hand. Add another amaryllis stem at an angle and continue to add the rest of the flowers and foliage.

4 Tie the arrangement securely with a length of raffia or garden string. Treat the amaryllis stems with care, as they may split under too much pressure.

5 Cut the stems at an angle so they are roughly the same length and will all be able to sit in water. If the arrangement is well balanced, it should be able to stand unaided. If the bouquet is a gift to someone, stand it in water until you present it.

INSIDER TIP

• **Amaryllis stems are fragile** and the flower heads they carry are heavy, so the stems can easily split if you hold them too tightly. Buy stems that are as fresh as possible with the buds just opening so the flower heads don't splay out in the arrangement.

Flowers and foliage

← 5 ruby red single roses

↓ 7 'Red Lion' amaryllis

5 'Tamango' spray roses ↓

← 7 'Dolly Parton' hypericum stems

10 berried ivy stems →

Other materials

Florist's scissors
Raffia or garden string

Possible substitutions

Lilies (for amaryllis); eryngium (for spray roses); trachelium (for hypericum); gerberas (for single roses)

WINTER WEDDING

These romantic yet restrained wedding arrangements are deliberately ordered and formal, but with a twist: a mass of tiny frosted pearls are hidden in the boutonniere and bouquet. It's worth showing the bride how to hold her bouquet correctly: its weight should draw her arms down naturally so they are straighter, allowing the flowers to be shown off at the best angle.

BOUTONNIERE

1 stem white spray roses
1 ivy stem
Wired pearls (available from
  haberdashers, bead shops, and
  specialty flower markets)

BOUQUET

9 white spray roses
9 white single 'Avalanche' roses
11 white freesias
7 white trachelium
5 white lisianthus
11 eucalyptus stems
Wired pearls (available from
  haberdashers, bead shops, and
  specialty flower markets)

TABLE CENTERPIECE

10 white spray roses
12 white single 'Avalanche' roses
12 white freesias
11 white trachelium
6 eucalyptus stems
6 ivy stems

PEW END

8 white single roses

← white spray roses

← white lisianthus

↑ white freesias

↓ white single 'Avalanche' roses

↓ eucalyptus stems

↓ ivy stems

↑ white trachelium

BOUTONNIERE

Sprays of wired pearls tucked in between delicate spray roses are a charming detail that lifts this boutonniere out of the ordinary.

1 Wire the roses and ivy leaves according to the step-by-steps for wiring a boutonniere in section 1 (pp48–51). Gather several wired pearls into a spray and bind the wires together with stem tape.

2 Group the individual roses, arrange the wired pearls around them, and encircle them all with the ivy leaves. Trim the wires so they are graduated, wrap stem tape around all the wires, and press the tape down with your fingers to seal it.

3 Mist the roses occasionally to keep them fresh until they are needed, then supply the boutonniere with a pearl-tipped pin to attach it onto the lapel of a jacket.

BOUQUET

This bouquet is a large spiral-stemmed design with pearls scattered through it. It has a high binding point to give a compact look.

1 Divide the different ingredients into separate piles. Hold a rose and add one of each of the ingredients at an angle to create a spiral effect. Turn the bunch in the same direction as you work, and add lengths of wired pearls.

2 Add all the blooms in turn so that they are balanced equally throughout the bunch. Arrange the last two layers of flowers slightly lower around the edges to create a domed effect.

3 Secure the bunch with a length of raffia or string. Trim the stem ends with garden shears. If you want to cover the stems with ribbon, wind a long length of white ribbon down around the stems and up again. Tie the two ends together in a small knot and press pearl pins in a vertical line into the ribbon to secure it and create a pretty detail. Mist the flowers occasionally until needed.

TABLE CENTERPIECE

Each stem of this table centerpiece needs to be inserted at an angle to cover the foam and give a smooth, rounded shape. When you have placed all the flowers and foliage, move the arrangement into position, place a large white candle in the center, and cover it with a hurricane glass.

1 Soak a 12in-wide (30cm) floral foam ring briefly in water.

2 Arrange the ivy stems and angle them downward to create a graduated shape from the center to the edge of the ring (there is no need to cover the inside of the ring, as the glass will sit in the center). Angle the stems around the outside edge of the ring upward so they hide the tray.

3 Add stems of eucalyptus in between the ivy to create a sparse but even coverage of foliage.

4 Add the single roses, distributing them evenly. Group the spray roses and freesias as you angle them into the foam so they create more impact. Insert the trachelium in a uniform pattern. Then position the ring and add the candle and glass.

PEW END

1 Punch two holes in the top of a small bowl using a pair of scissors and insert a long length of wire through each hole. This wire is to tie around the end of the pew and attach the flowers securely.

2 Soak a third of a block of floral foam, shave about ½in (1cm) off the top and strap it onto the small bowl with diagonal strips of florist's tape. Trim the rose stems to about 4in (10cm), keeping just a few leaves at the top, and leave one rose stem slightly longer than the others (reserve the cut rose stems for later). Insert this tallest rose at the top of the foam.

3 Arrange the rest of the roses at an angle, with the shortest stems at the front to create a graduated, semi-domed effect. Trim the reserved cut stems to about 7in (18cm) and insert them into the base of the foam at angles that mirror those of the roses above.

4 Wrap a piece of cellophane around the foam to prevent the netting absorbing the water and sagging. There's no need to tape it, as the netting will keep it in place (pp204–205). Place a length of white netting underneath the small bowl and tie both ends in a large bow. Attach the arrangement to the pew end.

PEW END

This pew end, with its romantic cloud of netting tied in a bow, is designed to look like a hand-tied bouquet, though it is actually a floral foam arrangement. Roses don't last well out of water, so this rather unusual way of arranging them means they last longer; a real hand-tied bouquet of roses would quickly become floppy and unsightly. This also means you can arrange the pew ends the day before for convenience. The result is a slightly larger-scale, more dramatic, display: the impression given is that the roses are on longer stems than they really are.

SPECIAL EVENTS
Fresh flowers need to be fully open to look their best at a special event such as a wedding, so buy them a few days before you make the arrangements to ensure they will be in peak condition.

AMARYLLIS IN AN URN

The secret of this impressive, elegant front-facing vase arrangement is that it is incredibly simple: the grand scale and beauty of the design almost mask its minimalism (together the urn and birch twigs are 5ft (1.5m) high). The amaryllis will last without water for an evening if you want to use a non-watertight container, but will last for two weeks if you re-cut the stems and refresh the water. This makes a stunning front-facing display in an entrance hall or on a buffet table.

HOW TO ARRANGE

1 Put the urn in position and arrange the birch twigs in a natural splay, with the shorter twigs around the outside and the taller twigs in the middle. Keep the look as informal and as natural as possible. The twigs can be as tall as you like for dramatic effect, but keep them in proportion to the size of the urn. Keep any birch twig off-cuts and add them to the sides of the design if needed.

2 Tuck the amaryllis stems inside the front edge of the urn so that the flower heads rest just above the neck of the container. Arrange a single layer of flowers around the rim and then build up a second tier of blooms in between them so that you create a double layer of flower heads.

3 If you have used a watertight container, fill it with water (amaryllis displace so much water due to their hollow stems that it is best to do this last).

Flowers and foliage

8 amaryllis →

3 bunches → natural birch twigs

AMARYLLIS BUDS
Choose amaryllis with some buds already open and some still closed to give shape and interest to this design.

Other materials

Large urn (18in/46cm high)

Possible substitutions

Hydrangeas or lilies (for amaryllis); birch twigs sprayed silver or white (for natural birch twigs)

AMARYLLIS TREE

This minimalist amaryllis tree is a sophisticated way of displaying a floral foam arrangement of flowers. If you don't have room for a real tree at Christmas, an arrangement such as this is the perfect alternative. Choose a streamlined opaque container or vase that is about half the size of the flower stems to get the right proportions (the steps in this project show a clear vase rather than the final black vase to reveal the construction of materials inside the vase). This arrangement is also ideal in a hallway or as a bar display at a party. It will last for seven days if you mist the flowers regularly and keep the floral foam wet.

Flowers

← 5 'Hercules' amaryllis

Other materials

Tall cube vase
Raffia
Florist's scissors
5 garden stakes
Cellophane
½ block floral foam
Craft knife
Seagrass (optional)
Black pebbles or gravel

Possible substitution

'Grand Prix' roses (use 15–20 stems)

HOW TO ARRANGE

1 Arrange the amaryllis stems in a bunch with straight stems and tie them with a length of raffia just below the base of the flower heads so the raffia remains hidden. Trim the ends of the stems to the same length.

2 Insert a garden stake inside each hollow amaryllis stem. Each stake should be longer than the amaryllis stem. Trim the stakes so that they are all the same length.

3 Pack the lower half of the vase with scrunched-up cellophane or recycled plastic bags (this means you don't have to use a large block of foam—half of which would be wasted—which would also cause the vase to become very heavy). Fill three-quarters of the vase with water. Trim the soaked block of floral foam so it fits the diameters of the vase and put it into position.

4 Push the amaryllis stems and garden stakes down into the foam until the stakes disappear from view and the flowers can stand unaided.

INSIDER TIPS

• **Cut or tear off the small brown sepals** around the base of each amaryllis flower head, as they wither and look unattractive if they are left on the flower.

• **Amaryllis stems** draw up lots of water when they stand in a bucket or vase because their stems are hollow. When you take out the flowers to recut and arrange them, be careful that the water inside the stems doesn't flood out and cause any damage.

• **The buds on amaryllis stems** open up in sequence, so you can carefully cut off the older blooms when they are past their best to make room for the newer buds to open up.

5 Fill the rest of the vase with black pebbles up to the brim. These pebbles will also help to support the flower stems. Then top up the vase with water. Tie a length of seagrass neatly around the fixed stems as an extra detail, if you wish.

6 If you have any stems of amaryllis left over, cut the stems short and arrange the flowers in a short black vase to stand alongside the main arrangement. Alternatively, make up separate stems in small vases as individual place settings for a meal.

LUSH WINTER MIX

This luxurious, very full vase arrangement is an all-around (rather than front-facing) display that would look wonderful on a circular table in the center of a large entrance hall or conservatory. The mix of classically wintery red and silvery green hues is freshened up with exotic pale-pink cymbidium orchids, arching stems of lime-green molucella, and green tie leaves that line the inside of the vase and conceal the stems. Use chicken wire if you find it hard to angle the stems (p37). The flowers will last well for seven to 10 days (pp34–35).

HOW TO ARRANGE

1 The central vein, or midrib, of a green tie leaf can break and spoil the visual effect of lining a vase, so use a craft knife or scissors to slice down either side of the midrib of each green tie leaf and separate the leaf into two separate halves. Curl the half-leaves around the inside of the vase in diagonal patterns.

2 Trim the stems of ruscus just a little so that they give height to the display, and arrange them in the vase to create a three-dimensional fan shape. Then add the eucalyptus. To create an all-around arrangement, keep turning the vase around as you work to build up an even shape from every angle.

3 Be aware of the sharp white spikes left on the stems of molucella when you strip off the leaves; cut these spikes off, too, so they don't stand in water. Recut the stems just above a join, or node, and arrange them in the center of the vase, turning the vase around as you work.

4 Arrange the roses next and then the orchids, as they are the most dominant flowers. Place them in the obvious gaps around the arrangement. Check that you have an even, graduated shape from every angle, then put the vase in position and top it up almost to the rim with water.

EXOTIC ADDITION
Cymbidium orchids with roses may appear an unlikely mix, but the different colors and shapes of these blooms actually enhance one another.

Flowers and foliage

6 single red roses ↓

← 6 molucella

↓ 7 ruscus stems

← 5 pale pink cymbidium orchids

← 2 green tie leaves

← 7 'Baby Blue' eucalyptus stems

Other materials

Flared clear glass vase (12in/30cm high)
Florist's scissors
Chicken wire (optional)

Possible substitutions

Euphorbia (for molucella), amaryllis (for roses), eucalyptus (for ruscus)

WINTER FANTASY

A show-stopping display such as this works as a sophisticated focal point for any winter celebration, and is easy to achieve: bare birch twigs, echoing the dormant season, are trimmed to a length that suits the height of the heavy metal urn and then arranged in a natural splay. Upended amaryllis flowers are attached to the twigs with 22 gauge wire that has been threaded through the base of each stem. The hollow stems are filled with water to keep them alive.

EFFECT The grand scale of these arching, spreading twigs contained within the "tree trunk" of the urn, and the unusual arrangement of amaryllis, create a sense of drama and delight.

SHAPE This arrangement, with its mass of tall twigs, represents the shape of a bare tree in winter. The amaryllis flowers hanging from its branches are reminiscent of decorations on a Christmas tree.

COLOR White amaryllis flower heads and brown twigs are used to create a wintry feel. When the flowers are past their best, they can be replaced with fresh white amaryllis.

SECTION THREE
ALL YEAR-ROUND

While seasonal flowers and foliage come and go, all-year-round blooms are a staple that you can rely on to create stunning designs any time.

ROSEBUD CIRCLET

Sometimes a simple wired circlet of roses is just what is needed to complete a small child's party outfit, or to adorn their head at a Christmas or midsummer celebration. It is also perfect as a young bridesmaid's headdress for a wedding. If you want to make the circlet the day before, it will remain in good condition as long as you give the roses a long drink of water and seal each bud well with stem tape after you have wired it (the buds all need to be wired so that they face the same way). Give the ivy a drink too, as its stem won't be sealed with stem tape. Try to keep the sequence of closed and semi-open buds quite random as you attach them to the wire frame to create a loose arrangement of blooms. The circlet should stay fresh for up to 24 hours if misted with water.

Flowers and foliage

← 4 small pink spray roses, in bud and semi-open

← 1–2 trailing ivy stems

HOW TO ARRANGE

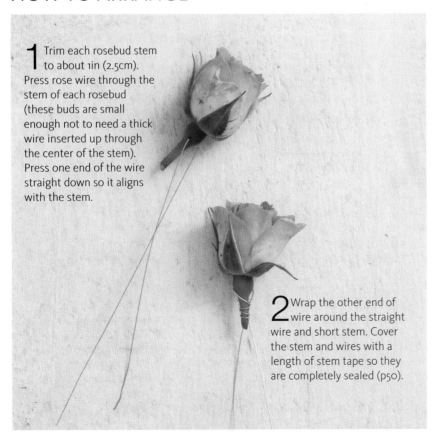

1 Trim each rosebud stem to about 1in (2.5cm). Press rose wire through the stem of each rosebud (these buds are small enough not to need a thick wire inserted up through the center of the stem). Press one end of the wire straight down so it aligns with the stem.

2 Wrap the other end of wire around the straight wire and short stem. Cover the stem and wires with a length of stem tape so they are completely sealed (p50).

Other materials

Florist's scissors
Silver rose wire
22 gauge wire
Stem tape

Possible substitution

Mini carnations

3 To make the frame for the circlet, measure the child's head with a length of string first.

4 Then arrange several lengths of 22 gauge wire in a line so they are the same length in total as the string and slightly overlap each other. Incorporate a little extra length for small hooks to be made at either end.

5 Cover the overlapping wires with stem tape.

6 Seal the ends and trim off any excess tape.

7 Make a small hook at either end of the taped wire frame.

8 Place a wired, taped rosebud at one end of the frame and wind stem tape around the wired end only; the stem must remain free to be angled correctly, so it should not be attached to the frame. Bind all the wired rosebuds to the frame in the same way.

9 Interlock the wire hooks and press them together to secure them.

11 Mist the rosebuds and ivy regularly, particularly if it is hot, to keep them as fresh as possible until the circlet is used. You can also cover the circlet loosely with damp tissue to retain its freshness for longer.

10 Interweave a length of trailing ivy loosely between the rosebuds.

EXOTICS IN A BOX

Exotic flowers and foliage always look sculptural and architectural. To give this hand-tied bouquet a natural feel it is arranged in a wooden box intended to mimic the textural bark of coconut trees. If you prefer to keep to clean lines and smooth surfaces, display the flowers in a glass container, and feel free to choose your own combination of tropical flowers and foliage. This design will look good on a table in a contemporary setting and will last for seven days or so if you keep the flowers in good condition (pp34–35).

HOW TO ARRANGE

1 Take each black tie leaf and make short slashes with a craft knife on either side of the midrib (the central vein running along the length of the leaf blade).

2 Sort the different flowers and foliage into separate piles. Hold a ginger lily in one hand and add an anthurium to it, twisting the stems around slightly in one direction in your hand. Add more stems at the same angle to create a spiral stem effect. Turn the arrangement slightly in the same direction as you work.

3 Leave a few protea stems aside and insert the remaining flowers and foliage at a lower angle around the edges of the bunch to create a domed effect. As you add a black tie leaf, pull the tip of the leaf down to the binding point with one hand so the separated sections curl over. Secure the stems and the tips of the black tie leaves together with raffia.

4 Pack cellophane around the vase in the box to make it secure. Fill the vase with water and place the bunch in it. Add the last few protea around the edges of the vase to echo the square shape of the box and cover the cellophane. Wrap seagrass cord around the box and tie it in a neat knot.

BLACK TIE LEAVES
The three separated sections of this slashed leaf create a ribbon-like effect.

Flowers and foliage

← 5 'African King' anthuriums

← 8 orange and yellow protea

↓ 3 red ginger lilies

1 orange → heliconia

2 umbrella → grass

10 black → tie leaves

Other materials

Wooden box (14 x 14in/36 x 36cm and 10in/25cm deep) with a vase inside
Craft knife
Raffia
Florist's scissors
Cellophane
Seagrass cord

Possible substitutions

Strelitzia (for ginger lilies); Singapore orchids (for protea)

ARCHITECTURAL LEAVES
Some leaves are visually striking and add a dramatic element to a display of big, bold flowers. These umbrella grasses and green tie leaves provide strong, clean lines and interest.

TOWERING LIATRIS

Liatris buds open from the tip down, so their bright lilac color appears to stream down the length of their stems to give this floral foam design a wonderfully atmospheric effect. The liatris are just a little longer than the height of the container, which gives the display as much drama as possible without looking too top-heavy. This design would suit a contemporary hallway or room; several identical displays, or smaller versions surrounding this arrangement, would make a stylish variation. It should last for seven to 10 days if you keep the foam wet.

HOW TO ARRANGE

1 Pack some scrunched-up cellophane or plastic bags inside the vase until it is about two-thirds full (p212).

2 Trim a soaked block of floral foam so that it fits snugly inside the vase just below the rim.

3 Trim the liatris stems so they are all the same length (about 20–22in/50–55cm). Press the stems firmly into the foam in straight lines, placing them as close to each other as possible, and working from the front of the vase to the back. Twist the stems slightly as you press them in so that they stand as straight as possible and don't flare out to the sides. Liatris require very little aftercare once they have been arranged, so just mist the flowers occasionally.

LINES OF LIATRIS
The liatris should be placed firmly and methodically in straight lines; don't keep pulling them out to rearrange them, or the floral foam will start to disintegrate.

Flowers

← 50 liatris

Other materials

Tall black cube vase (16½in/42cm high)
Cellophane or plastic bags
1 block floral foam
Craft knife
Florist's scissors

Possible substitutions

Aconitum or gentian

ALL-YEAR-ROUND FANTASY

Many flower varieties, including lilies, roses, and orchids, are now available throughout the year, so to turn them into exciting arrangements it's worth choosing really bold, dynamic color mixes that provide interest, texture, and depth. The deliberate choice of a shocking pink urn heightens the powerful visual effect of this large, full display of concentrated pink and red blooms, which is off-set by long stems of dark green foliage.

EFFECT The idea of this design is to create maximum impact: these intensely colored flowers have many different shapes and textures that together create an impressive visual display.

SHAPE The smooth symmetrical curves of the large urn are an extreme contrast to the flared arrangement of diversely shaped buds, fully opened blooms, and feathered foliage.

COLOR The strong pink glassware is complemented by bright reds and deep pinks, and all are accentuated by the contrasting dark green color of the French ruscus.

CALLA LILIES

This impressive, pared-down display of flowers and foliage is designed to stand off-center inside a clear vase to accentuate its modern look. Several of these vase arrangements positioned in a line would make a fantastic statement; you could even vary the sizes of the vases so that the final vase is large enough to contain a whole arrangement inside it. If the birch twigs are in leaf when you buy them, just strip all the leaves off before you tie the twigs together. This display, with its unusual focus and height, looks fabulous in a hallway, hotel lobby, or in the corner of a room. As the bound calla lily stems are hard to recut, make sure they have a long drink of water before you arrange them.

HOW TO ARRANGE

1 Tie the bunched twigs together tightly about 3in (7.5cm) from the base with a length of raffia. Tie another length of raffia two-thirds of the way up the bunch, leaving the tips of the stems quite frothy and loose. Tie one more length of raffia midway between these two bindings. Trim the twigs straight across at the base so that they can stand upright in the vase.

2 Arrange three of the lilies in a horizontal row against the side of the twigs and bind the stems to the twigs just below the lily heads with more raffia. This length of raffia should cover the uppermost binding around the twigs.

3 Turn the bunch of twigs round slightly to the right and arrange another three lilies in a row. The bases of these lily heads should sit just above the central binding point of the twigs. Their stems should also adjoin the first three lily stems so that they all align and conceal the twigs beneath. Attach these lilies with a length of raffia that covers the binding around the twigs.

4 Turn the bunch of twigs slightly to the right once more and arrange three more lilies in a row so their heads sit just above the lowest binding near the base of the twigs. Ensure that these three lilies adjoin the other lily stems, then bind them with raffia. Trim all the lily stalks straight across so they are the same length as the birch twigs.

5 Fill the column vase with a little water and add a sterilizing tablet or flower food. Place the bound flowers and twigs inside. The protruding shapes of the lilies should naturally push the arrangement slightly off-center in the vase.

Flowers and foliage

9 yellow calla → lilies

← 1 bunch birch twigs

Other materials

Clear glass column vase
  (20in/51cm high)
Raffia
Florist's scissors
Sterilizing tablet or flower food

Possible substitutions

Arum lilies or ginger lilies (for calla lilies), bamboo (for birch twigs)

ASIAN FAN

This graphic, fan-shaped vase arrangement is simple to arrange and makes a stylish impact as a table centerpiece at a cocktail party, in an office boardroom, or in contemporary surroundings. It has an added element of fun that plays visual games with what you think you see: the floral foam "pebbles", when threaded onto snake grass stems, look identical to stone pebbles. Use these foam pebbles only as an optional extra—their absence won't detract from the arrangement. It will last for three to five days if you refresh the water.

HOW TO ARRANGE

1 Place a pin holder at the back of the container. Arrange the tall calla lilies first to create a high focal point: trim the stems and press them into the middle of the pin holder so they stand at slightly different heights.

2 Trim the rose stems so that the sprays are slightly shorter than the lowest calla lily. Snip off a few single stems and reserve them. Arrange the main rose stems at the front of the pin holder, then fill any obvious gaps with the single stems.

3 Place the end of each snake grass stem behind the lilies in the back of the pin holder. If you are using soaked foam pebbles, thread them onto the snake grass stems. Bend the stems once or twice in the center and place the thin top end back on the pin holder or against the edge of the container to create a spreading effect from the center of the arrangement.

4 Divide the bear grass into bunches of 5 or 6 stems, bind them with elastic bands, and place them around the arrangement on the pin holder to pull the design together. Scatter two handfuls of black pebbles in the container to hide the pin holder and add enough water to cover the bases of the stems.

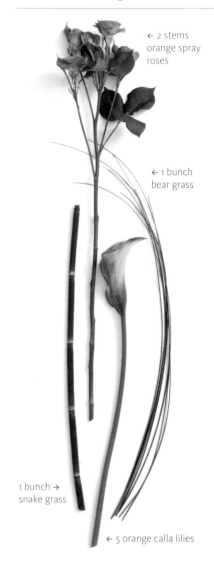

Flowers and foliage

← 2 stems orange spray roses

← 1 bunch bear grass

1 bunch → snake grass

← 5 orange calla lilies

FOAM PEBBLES
It's easiest to thread these foam pebbles onto the stems of the snake grass after soaking them briefly in water.

Other materials

Wide, shallow column container (5in/13cm high, 12in/30cm wide)
1 pin holder
Florist's scissors
Foam pebbles (optional)
Black pebbles

Possible substitutions

Alliums or nerines (for calla lilies); tracheliums or peonies (for roses); thin bamboo (for snake grass); lily grass or china grass (for bear grass)

GREEN BOUQUET

With its limited, neutral palette of hues, this hand-tied bouquet suits any room, whether colorful or pristine white. It is also an ideal gift for someone who might prefer a more contemporary arrangement. As it will last well in harsh temperatures such as fierce air-conditioning or hot rooms, it is a suitable choice for the office or an apartment. This arrangement will not lose any of its impact if you only use three varieties of green flowers. You could choose all white, red, or pink flowers, too, for an equally vibrant display. The bouquet will last a week if you keep the flowers in good condition (pp34–35).

HOW TO ARRANGE

1 Sort the different flowers and foliage into separate piles. Hold the stem of one flower in your hand and add another variety of flower to it at an angle, twisting the bunch around slightly in one direction in your hand as you do so.

2 Add one of each of all the flowers and leaves at the same angle to create a spiral stem effect, turning the bunch in the same direction as you do so. Reserve most of the green tie leaves until the end. As you add the green tie leaves, fold the tips of the leaves over and hold them at the binding point. This helps to provide an unusual, interesting feature and added texture. Check that you are happy with the arrangement of flowers, then add the remaining blooms. Insert the last two layers of flowers at a lower angle around the edges to create a domed effect, and add the remaining green tie leaves last.

3 Tie the arrangement with garden string or raffia secured in a knot.

4 Cut the stems at an angle, so they are roughly the same length and will all be able to sit in water. If the bouquet is a gift, wrap it and tie it with a black, green, or cream ribbon (pp54–55).

Flowers and foliage

6 shamrock → chrysanthemums

↓ 15 single roses

↓ 7 green santini

5 green → anthurium

↑ 8 green tie leaves

Other materials

Garden string or raffia
Florist's scissors

Possible substitutions

Hydrangeas (for shamrock chrysanthemums); small spray roses (for santini); gerberas (for antirrhinum)

ORCHID CHAIR-BACK

Simple hand-tied bouquets attached to the back of every chair at a celebration meal make a lovely feature. They can also provide the finishing touches to a special event such as a wedding, Christmas dinner, or summer garden party. This chair-back has been arranged using the spiral hand-tied bouquet technique, but instead of having a domed appearance it is designed to be front-facing, as your guests will view the flowers more often from the front or the side than from above. As the flowers are out of water, they will only last a few hours.

HOW TO ARRANGE

1 Give the orchids a drink, as they will be out of water for the duration of the event. Cut their long stems in the middle to create two separate, short stems.

2 Hold an orchid stem in one hand and add a few stems around it at the binding point. Insert each stem at an angle to create a spiral effect. There is no need to turn the bunch each time, as you want the flowers to all face forward. Place the longer stems at the back and the shorter stems at the front.

3 Check that you are happy with the arrangement of flowers, then tie them at the binding point with a length of raffia. Cut the ends of the stems straight across to neaten them up.

4 Wrap a long length of ribbon around the top of the chair-back and tie it in a knot at the back. Tie the bouquet onto the ribbon with a short piece of ribbon.

5 Cut one last long piece of ribbon and wrap it around the bouquet at the binding point (to cover the raffia and any visible knots). Secure the ribbon in a bow and allow the loose ends to trail down the back of the chair.

STREAMLINED DESIGN
To keep the arrangement aligned with the chair-back, wrap reel wire around a couple of stems and tie the ends onto the chair.

Flowers

6 lime green → Singapore orchid stems

3 purple → Singapore orchid stems

Other materials

Florist's scissors
Raffia
Wide ribbon
Reel wire (optional)

Possible substitution

Spray roses

WALLPAPER ORCHIDS

This exquisitely delicate design is an ideal way to display the flower heads of an orchid plant if they are just past their best. Orchid petals look a little like butterfly wings, and in this slim, nearly two-dimensional vase arrangement the wired orchids appear to almost flutter up and down the sides of the transparent glass as they float in the water. A front-facing display like this looks stunning in a modern kitchen, bathroom, hallway, hotel lobby, or on a back-lit shelf. The orchids should last for three days before they become waterlogged.

HOW TO ARRANGE

1 Fill the vase with about 4in (10cm) of water initially and add a sterilizing tablet or flower food.

2 Cut the orchid flowers off the main stem so that just a short stalk remains at the base of each flower. Cut a length of colored wire about 8in (20cm) long. Choose pink wire to match the orchids. Make a small hook at one end and place the hook against the side of one of the flower stalks. Wind the length of wire gently two or three times around the stalk, taking care not to slice through it. Handle the orchids with care so that you don't bruise the petals.

3 When you have wired all the orchids, cut several more lengths of colored wire and individually wrap them around two of your fingers. Pull them out slightly to create a loose spiral effect. These spiral wires create a framework for the orchids to sit on to prevent them falling to the bottom of the vase.

4 Place a few spiral wires in the vase and add some orchids on top: place the orchid head in the vase first so that it faces outward, and position the wire behind it. Use a clean stick to reposition any flowers that move. Build up layers of orchids and spiral wires (adding water to the top of each layer) in a random pattern to the top of the vase, then fill the vase to the rim with water.

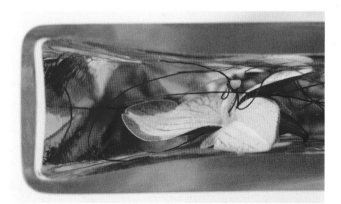

WIRED STALKS
Orchid stalks are very fragile, which is why you need to place the wire hook against the stem, not around it, when wiring these blooms. Use a stick to reposition any flowers that may have moved.

Flowers

↓ 2 pink phalaenopsis orchid stems

Other materials

Thin, clear column glass vase (15in/39cm high and 2½in/6.5cm wide) or fishbowl or square cube (with the flowers facing outward)
Sterilizing tablet or flower food
Florist's scissors
Colored decorative reel wire

Possible substitution

Singapore orchid heads

CARNATION POMANDER

This most adaptable of floral foam arrangements can be hung from an overhanging tree branch above an outdoor table set for lunch or dinner in summer or carried by a young bridesmaid during a wedding ceremony. Several identical pomanders can be hung like tree baubles around a living room at Christmas or laid as individual place settings with the ribbons trailing across the table for a celebration dinner (and then taken home by guests as gifts at the end of the evening). The pomanders will last for a couple of days if you give them an occasional misting with water.

Flowers

25 green → carnations

HOW TO ARRANGE

1 Make a hook at one end of a length of wire. The wire should be longer than the diameter of the floral foam ball.

2 Cut two lengths of ribbon—one thick, one thin—about 8in (20cm) long. Lay the thin ribbon on the thick ribbon, fold them over, and press the ends together. Place the wire hook around the ribbon ends and press it down to secure them. Wrap one end of the wire around the wire hook and ribbon ends a few times.

3 Cover the base of the ribbons and the top of the wire in stem tape.

Other materials

Florist's scissors
90 gauge wire
Stem tape
Thick and thin ribbon
1 small floral foam ball
Small piece of garden stake

Possible substitutions

Spray or single rosebuds, or half-opened roses (pp108–111)

4 Push the end of the wire right through the center of a soaked foam ball so that the ribbon handle sits at the top of the ball.

5 Press a small piece of garden stake against the base of the ball where the wire extends out. Wind the free end of wire around the piece of stake to prevent the handle loosening or falling off. Cut off the excess wire.

6 Cut the stems off the carnations at the point—the top node—where the uppermost leaves grow. This should leave a very short stem of about 1in (2.5cm).

INSIDER TIPS

• **Water will leach out** of the floral foam as you arrange the flowers, so allow a little time to pass after you have finished working on the pomander so that any more water can drain out before you hang it up, place it on a table, or give it away.

• **Add some pearl-topped pins** to the center of each carnation flower head if you want to display the pomander for a special occasion or festive party.

• **Mist the carnations** with water to keep them fresh and the foam ball moist.

7 Starting at the top of the ball, press the flower stalks into the floral foam. It is important to work methodically, not randomly, pressing the flowers close enough to each other so that the foam is completely covered, but without crushing the flowers. Work either in a spiral from the top, or downward in sections. Cover the ball so that no gaps are visible.

CARNATION SCULPTURE

This very modern display of traditional flowers reveals an interesting juxtaposition of shapes and textures: the feathery clumps of carnation petals set in a round, floral foam ball contrast dramatically with the smooth-sided, angular vase that the ball sits on. Although it looks impressive, it is simple to make. It would look stunning in an entrance hall or on a bar at a party. If you need to decorate tables, make up some smaller versions as table centerpieces. It lasts for three to five days if you mist the flowers.

HOW TO ARRANGE

1 Check that the floral foam ball will sit securely on top of the vase, then soak it in water, place it on top of the vase, and press it down slightly so that it is as secure as possible.

2 Cut the stems off the carnations at the point, known as the top node, where the uppermost leaves grow. This should leave a short stem of about 1in (2.5cm).

3 Starting at the top of the ball, press the carnation flower stalks into the floral foam. Work methodically, not randomly, pressing the flowers close enough to each other so that the foam is completely covered and there are no gaps, but without crushing and bruising the flower petals. Work either in a spiral from the top, or downward in sections. Cover the whole ball so that no gaps are visible.

INSIDER TIPS

- **As with all floral foam arrangements**, give the carnations a long drink in deep water before you cut off the stems and arrange them in the foam.

- **Don't over-soak the foam ball**, or it will start to crumble and fall apart. Place the ball in a bucket of water, allow it to sink to the bottom, then lift it straight out.

Flowers

← 45–50 red carnations

Other materials

Tall opaque cube vase (16in/40cm high)
1 floral foam ball (7in/18cm in diameter)
Florist's scissors

Possible substitution

Hydrangeas

GERBERA IN LINES

A clean, modern display such as this could be classed as a "perpetual arrangement": the floral foam design is so easy to reinvent that you just pull out the old flowers and insert fresh blooms. Its fun, quirky appearance means that it would suit a kitchen windowsill or hall table, or brighten up the back of a table of food at a children's party. The aim is to create a tiered effect, with the tallest flowers at the back and the shortest at the front, but don't be obsessive about creating exact levels with each row of flowers. It will last for at least a week if you keep the floral foam moist.

HOW TO ARRANGE

1 As the flowers are arranged in foam, stand them in water for an hour or so after trimming their stems. If the container isn't watertight, line it with cellophane or a similar material. Place the soaked, trimmed foam blocks in the container.

2 Trim the stems of four gerberas to similar lengths and press them into the back of the foam so they are equal distances apart. These will be the tallest flowers in the display, so don't cut them too short.

3 Place another row of gerberas, with their stems cut slightly shorter, immediately in front of the first row.

4 Add the last row of gerberas at the front of the arrangement, placing each stem directly in front of the other pairs of gerberas. Then tie each set of tiered stems together with some brightly colored wire that is preferably the same color as the flower heads.

5 If you want to add an extra decorative touch to the ties, coil some lengths of wire into swirls (see below). Then scatter enough black pebbles over the surface of the container to completely cover the floral foam.

DECORATIVE SWIRLS
To make the wire swirls, bend a length of wire (about 1½in/3.5cm) 90° at one end of the wire and pinch and push it into the shape of a loop. Rotate the loop in your fingers to form a circle of wire around it. The circle should be tight enough so that the wires touch, or almost touch. Keep rotating the wire to form six or so circles that together create a swirl. Attach to the front of the stems using the short end of wire at the back of the swirl.

Flowers

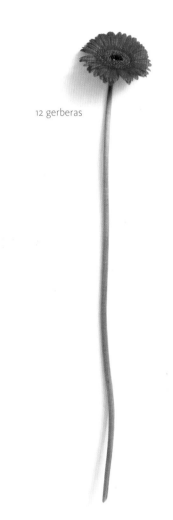

12 gerberas

Other materials

Glavanized metal trough
   (16in/41cm long, 6in/15cm deep),
   terra-cotta trough, or ceramic
   container
Florist's scissors
Cellophane (optional)
1–2 blocks floral foam
Colored decorative thick
   reel wire
Black pebbles, shells, or gravel

Possible substitution

Anthuriums

USEFUL ADDRESSES

You should be able to find the flowers used in this book in your local florists or pick them from your garden, but here are some useful addresses—websites, shops, and markets—that we recommend. Also listed here are floristry societies and organizations.

SOCIETIES AND ORGANIZATIONS

Here is a range of resources that offers information about all plants and flowers, and societies and courses.

WHOLESALE FLORIST & FLORIST SUPPLIER ASSOCIATION

www.wffsa.org
Floristry trade association with a website directory of wholesale florists available in your local area.

AMERICAN INSTITUTE OF FLORAL DESIGNERS

www.aifd.org
National organization devoted to recognizing and encouraging excellence in floral design, offering accreditation in the area floral design, as well as educational courses for non-members.

SOCIETY OF AMERICAN FLORISTS

www.safnow.org.
Information and advice on flowers and floral design, as well as a listing of florists by area.

FLORISTS' REVIEW

www.floristsreview.com
The oldest and largest trade publication for the floral industry. The magazine is published monthly.

AMERICAN HORTICULTURAL SOCIETY

www.ahs.org
For information about all flowers and plants.

CANADIAN INSTITUTE OF FLORAL DESIGN

www.proflorists.net
For a range of courses in floristry.

FLOWERS CANADA

flowerscanada.org
Information on floral design, and a listing of local florists.

ROYAL BOTANICAL GARDENS

www.rbg.ca
Canada's largest botanical garden, offering courses, workshops, and information.

FLOWER MARKETS

Check opening times before you visit flower markets and get there early to beat the rush.

BOSTON FLOWER EXCHANGE

www.thebostonflowerexchange.com
540 Albany Street
Boston, MA

CHELSEA WHOLESALE FLOWER MARKET

131 west 28th Street
New York, NY

LOS ANGELES FLOWER DISTRICT

www.laflowerdistrict.com
766 Wall Street
Los Angeles, CA 90014

SAN FRANCISCO WHOLESALE FLOWER MART

www.sfflmart.com
640 Brannan Street
San Francisco, CA 94107

ST. LAWRENCE MARKET

www.stlawrencemarket.com
Front and Jarvis Street
Toronto ON M5E 1C4

FLORISTS AND SUPPLIES

Florists often stock a range of supplies as well as fresh flowers. Ask your florist for what you're looking for and they should be able to help. Note that in the UK florists sometimes use water sterilization tablets for arrangements in clear vases. These tablets can be found at outdoor and/or camping supply stores. In the US, flower food often contains additives to deter bacteria growth and help to keep water clear.

FLORAL SUPPLIES
www.floralsupplies.com
For containers, floral supplies, floral foam, wires, and sundries.

WHOLESALE FLORAL
www.wholesalefloral.com
Online shop for vases, floral foam, ribbon, wire, and other materials.

FLORAL SUPPLY SYNDICATE
www.fss.com
For ribbons, vases, gift baskets, and decorative packaging supplies.

BLOOMS BY THE BOX
www.bloomsbythebox.com
Wide variety of wholesale flowers.

FLORISTS SUPPLY LTD.
www.floristssupply.com
Canadian supplier of wholesale flowers, floral foam, and other materials.

HOMEWARE STORES

Stores you'd usually think of for decorating a home also stock a range of containers and wires that are useful for floristry.

HOME DEPOT
www.homedepot.com
www.homedepot.ca
For vases and other containers.

LOWES
www.lowes.com
www.lowes.ca
For vases and other containers.

IKEA, US
www.ikea.com/us
Range of utility glassware and containers.

IKEA, CANADA
www.ikea.com/ca

TARGET
www.target.com
Large assortment of glassware and ceramics.

LEE VALLEY
www.leevalley.com
Mail-order and retail supplier of floral and indoor gardening materials.

INDEX

ACKNOWLEDGMENTS

THE AUTHORS WOULD LIKE TO THANK
Our fabulous team at Bloomsbury Flowers especially Megan, Gemma, Janet, Grace, Russ, and Anton.

Susannah Steel for putting our ramblings into coherent text and Jessie for being completely delightful and very patient.

Our wonderful photographer, Carolyn Barber, who is a complete inspiration and a joy to work with.

The team at Dorling Kindersley, including Mary-Clare Jerram for commissioning the book, Caroline de Souza, Dawn Henderson, Christine Keilty, Marianne Markham, Andrew Roff, and William Hicks.

All our suppliers at the New Covent Garden Flower Market as well as MHG Flowers and Metz.

DORLING KINDERSLEY WOULD LIKE TO THANK
Nicky Collings for art directing the photoshoot, Kate Davis for assisting with the photography, Steve Crozier for his retouching work, Sue Morony for proof-reading, and Hilary Bird for the index.

PICTURE CREDITS
All images © Dorling Kindersley
For further information see: www.dkimages.com

NOTE
Lily pollen is poisonous to cats and dogs, so if you own one, ensure that you remove all the pollen from the lilies before you arrange them.